THE ECONOMIC SYSTEM OF MEXICO

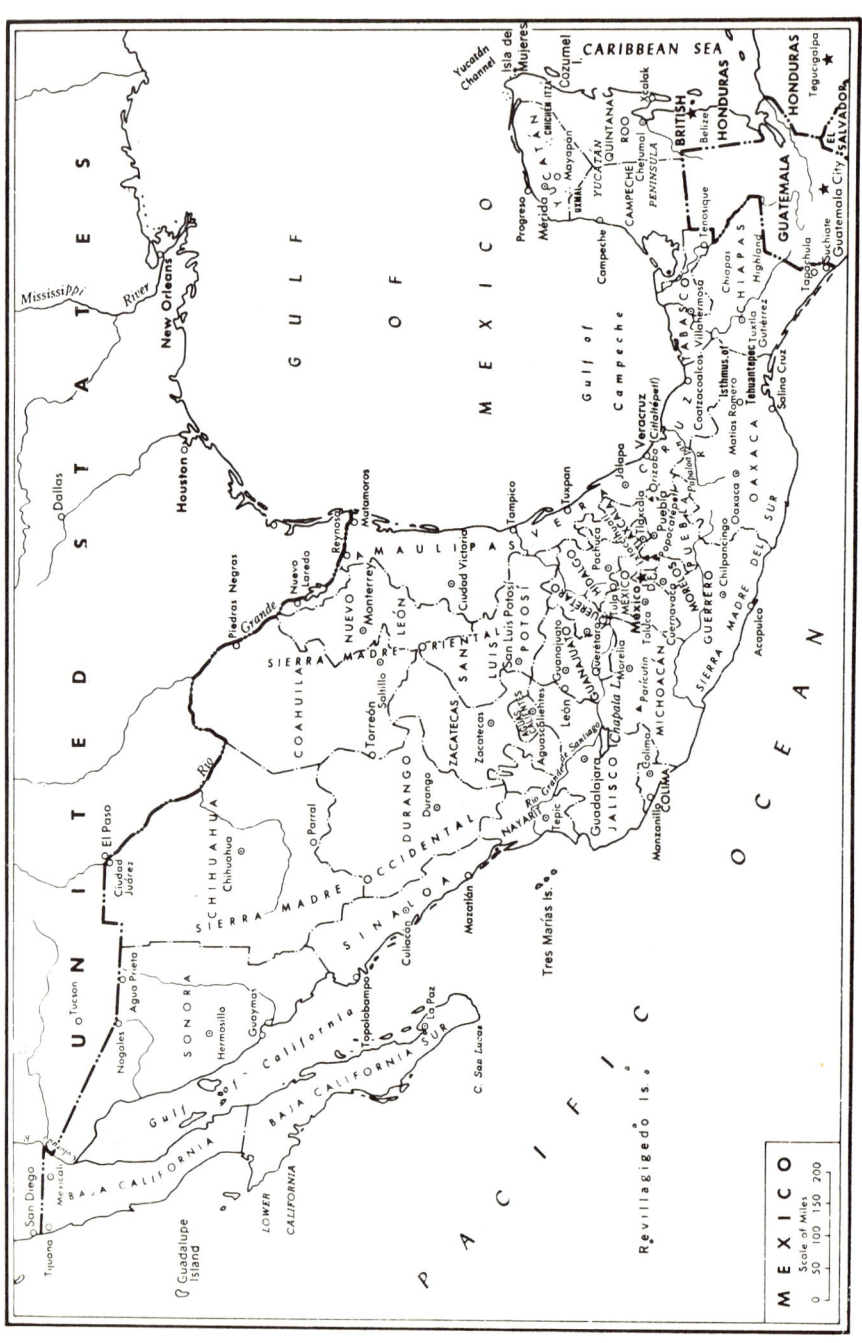

THE ECONOMIC SYSTEM OF MEXICO

John B. Ross

California Institute of International Studies
Stanford, California

Copyright © 1971, by
California Institute of International Studies

Library of Congress Catalog Card Number: 70-169794

International Standard Book Number: 912098-09-0

LIBRARY
FLORIDA STATE UNIVERSITY
TALLAHASSEE, FLORIDA

For Jocie, Beth, and Kurt

CONTENTS

PREFACE — xi

I. THE AGRICULTURAL SECTOR — 1

Land Tenure System — 1
The Agrarian Sector of the Partido Revolucionario Institucional (PRI) — 6
Government Intervention in Financing Agricultural Development — 7
Government Intervention in the Pricing and Marketing Process — 21
Summary — 26

II. THE INDUSTRIAL SECTOR — 35

Channels for Communication and Consultation between the Government and Business — 36
The Legal Basis for Promoting Industrial Development — 37
Import Controls — 41
The Mexicanization of Industry — 41
Nationalization — 43
Financing the Industrial Sector — 46
Concentration of Industry — 53
Summary — 58

III. THE FINANCIAL SYSTEM — 65

Structure of the Financial System — 65
Official Channel for Communication with the Government — 67
The Financial System and Economic Growth — 68
Summary — 78

IV. ECONOMIC GROWTH AND HUMAN WELFARE — 81

The Distribution of Income — 81
The Labor Sector of the PRI — 87
Minimum Wage Legislation — 89
Social Security — 92
The Government Budget and the Economy — 94
Education — 104
The Popular Sector of the PRI — 104
Summary and Conclusions — 105

BIBLIOGRAPHY	115
INDEX	126

TABLES

1	Dotación of Land to Ejidos by Presidential Periods	3
2	Distribution of Nongovernment-Owned Land in Mexico by Ejidos and Private Owners, and by Land Classification, 1940, 1950, and 1960	5
3	Occupational Structure of Mexico	8
4	Distribution of Gross National Product by Type of Economic Activity, 1940-69	10
5	Gross Public Fixed Investment for Agricultural Development, 1940-70	12
6	Accumulated Land Area Benefited by Government Irrigation Projects, 1940-68	15
7	Financing by Mexican Credit Institutions for Agricultural Production, 1942-69	19
8	Cost of Foodstuffs Index in Mexico City Sixteen Articles at Retail Price	23
9	Production of Maize, Wheat, and Beans in Mexico, 1940-67	24
10	Index of Industrial Production, 1945-69	44
11	Gross Public Fixed Investment for Industrial Development, 1940-70	47
12	Financing by the Mexican Banking System for Industrial Production, 1942-69	51
13	Total Financing Channeled through the Nacional Financiera, 1940-67	54
14	Activities of El Fondo de Garantía y Fomento a la Industria Mediana y Pequeña, 1954-69	57
15	Money Supply and Fixed-Interest Securities Outstanding, 1940-69	69

16	Financing Extended by National Credit Institutions, 1942-65	73
17	Financing Extended by Private Credit Institutions, 1942-65	75
18	Resources of the Private and Public Credit Institutions, 1945-69	77
19	GNP, in 1950 Pesos, and Population, 1940-70	82
20	Distribution of Family Income in Mexico, 1950 and 1957	84
21	Distribution of Personal Money Income from Wages and Salaries, 1950, 1956, and 1964-65	86
22	National Average of Minimum Daily Wages in Mexico for Urban and Rural Areas, 1940-65	91
23	Persons Insured by the Instituto Mexicano del Seguro Social, 1944-67	93
24	Total Receipts and Expenditures of the Instituto Mexicano del Seguro Social, 1944-67	95
25	Receipts of the Federal Government by Principal Sources, 1940-64	98
26	GNP, Actual Budgetary Expenditures, and Gross Fixed Investment, 1940-69	99
27	Ratios of Actual Budgetary Expenditures and Gross Fixed Investment to the GNP, 1940-67	102

PREFACE

In recent years, there has been a systematic examination of various national economies throughout the world.[1] Professor Calvin B. Hoover's article, "The Relevance of the Competitive, Laissez-faire Economic Model to Modern Capitalistic National Economies,"[2] has provided the general framework for analyzing the nonauthoritarian economies. In particular, answering the following questions posed in that article has been the major task of, and unifying factor in, the various descriptive analyses done thus far:

1. What industries have been nationalized (or denationalized) since the beginning of World War II (or other appropriate date)?
2. To what extent have cartel-type agreements in industry increased or decreased in importance during the period?
3. To what extent has concentration in industry been intensified?
4. To what extent have new forms of competition developed and offset oligopolistic tendencies or tendencies toward impairment of traditional forms of competition?
5. What currents and countercurrents with respect to governmental measures to further national economic self-sufficiency have been in operation during the period?
6. What is the present status and the trend with respect to governmental control of prices (including subsidy arrangements) and production in agriculture?
7. Has the extent to which the government takes responsibility for the stabilization of particular prices and the general price level changed significantly during the period?
8. To what extent has governmental responsibility for the maintenance of full employment affected the character of the system?
9. Are there more or less formal agreements among industry, labor organizations, and the government with respect to allowable increases in wages in relation to costs of living or in relation to the general price level or to the level of export prices?
10. Has there been any noticeable trend with respect to the extent to which the managements of industrial corporations act independently of effective control by stockholders?
11. Have there been pronounced changes in the degree of inequality in the distribution of national income and what have been the major causal factors in this change if it has occurred?
12. How substantial have been increases in and extensions of social security benefits during the period?
13. What changes have taken place with respect to the proportion of

national income which flows through the governmental budget?
14. To what extent has the government replaced private savers-investors as a source of capital funds for the national economy?
15. As a kind of "catch-all" question: To what extent has the national economy become a more or less "directed economy"? [3]

Studies of diverse economic systems have substantial practical as well as theoretical value. Governments around the world are being called upon—or have assumed the responsibility—to stimulate the rate of economic development, to assist in achieving an equitable distribution of income and wealth, and to assure that individual liberty is not forgotten in the drive for affluence. (Not all governmental intervention has succeeded in achieving these three goals.) Furthermore, economists are being asked not only to analyze various alternative means of attaining specified goals but are, with increasing frequency, in positions to assist in establishing goals.

There is considerable debate concerning the extent to which the basic structures of centrally planned economies and competitive, laissez faire economies are changing and becoming more similar. The revolution of rising expectations in less developed countries has engendered pressures on political leaders to find quick solutions to economic problems. Generally, this has meant that traditional doctrinaire approaches have been cast aside and various experiments, with differing degrees of state intervention, have been and are being undertaken. The actual accomplishments of many of these experiments have been disheartening.

Among less developed countries, Mexico has received increasing attention because of its record of economic achievement and political stability. In an effort to make a small contribution to the " 'grand design' for a series of studies of economic systems"[4] that Professor Hoover envisioned, I believed it important to examine the economic system of Mexico. I can only hope that this work will be a worthy component in his overall plan.

In general, I have used 1940 as the base year in this study. The year 1940 marked the end of President Cárdenas' term of office, with his primary concern for the agrarian masses, and the beginning of President Ávila Camacho's administration, which emphasized industrialization to a much greater degree.

It is the year in which the impact of World War II began to make itself felt, giving Mexico a major opportunity to begin realizing its industrial possibilities. It also marked the opening period in which the public official and the private businessman—despite periodic 'crises of confidence'—were obviously beginning to converse effectively across the ideological wall which once seemed to separate them.[5]

Where it seemed advisable, brief reference is made to events, economic conditions, and attitudes that occurred or prevailed prior to 1940. These references have, however, been kept to a minimum.

Mexico does publish a substantial volume of statistical data. Of course, there are instances where desired quantitative information is simply not available and where the accuracy of available data is questionable. I have made efforts, through personal contacts with various Mexican government officials, to assure, to the fullest extent possible, that the statistical series used in this study are internally consistent and adequately reflect the trend of important developments within the Mexican economy. The minimal use of official price indices was deliberate because of their limited coverage and reliability. There is little doubt that the official indices understate the actual price increases that have occurred. Fortunately, a new broader based and, hopefully, more sensitive national consumer price index has been developed.

I had the opportunity to travel in Mexico once as a student and recently as an officer of the Bank of America. During these trips, I visited various sections of the country and interviewed government officials, private businessmen, professional men, union and nonunion workers, *ejidatarios,* and owners of private agricultural units. While I am extremely thankful for the information and ideas that these individuals so freely gave me, I am not listing their names, as many expressed a preference to remain anonymous.

Unless otherwise indicated, I have translated all direct quotations from Spanish sources. Value figures are given in Mexican pesos, but U.S. dollar equivalents are provided in several instances to aid the reader. The value of the Mexican peso has changed a number of times since 1940. The Mexican peso equivalent per U.S. dollar was 5.50 pesos in 1940, approximately 4.85 pesos between 1941 and June 16, 1949, 8.65 pesos from June 17, 1949 to April 18, 1954, and 12.50 pesos since April 19, 1954.[6]

My debt to Professor Calvin B. Hoover cannot be recorded in a few sentences. I am deeply grateful for the intellectual stimulation, assistance, and encouragement he gave me as a graduate student of economics. It would have been impossible to have done this study without the financial assistance he provided in the form of a research assistantship and a travel grant that afforded me the opportunity to go to Mexico. His criticisms and suggestions have materially improved this study and have made me even more cognizant of the complexity and importance of studying economic systems.

Professor Robert S. Smith read the earlier drafts of this study. I was indeed fortunate to have the advice of a man of his recognized ability as an economist and skill as an editor. His death was a deeply felt loss to the economics profession.

In addition, I wish to acknowledge receiving financial assistance from Duke University in the form of a scholarship for one year and a fellowship during two years of my graduate education. I was also the recipient of a Ford Workshop Grant provided by the Ford Foundation and administered by Duke University. The Bank of America N.T. & S.A. gave me every possible assistance and encouragement to bring my dissertation to a successful conclusion and to rewrite and update it. I am especially grateful to Mrs. Marge Peterson, Mrs. Beverly Lankford, and Mrs. Valerie Johnson who carefully and cheerfully typed the early drafts of this study in spite of their already heavy work loads. Mrs. Claire Camiel typed my revised draft with speed and enthusiasm.

Special thanks are due to Professor Ronald Hilton of Stanford University, Executive Director of the California Institute of International Studies, who encouraged me to update and publish this work. For his patient but firm persistence in assuring that every fact and concept in the book was thoroughly re-examined, I am indeed grateful. His wife, Mary, was especially helpful about numerous editorial matters.

My wife, Jocie, made a substantial contribution to this study in innumerable ways, ranging from proofing the text and tables to assuring that our children were occupied in some room other than my study.

John B. Ross

San Francisco
March, 1971

Notes

1. Calvin B. Hoover, "The General Framework of the Studies," in *The Economic Systems of the Commonwealth*, pp. 3-4. In this article, Professor Hoover traces the fulfillment of his "grand design" for a systematic analysis of various economic systems.

2. *Kyklos*, fasc. 1 (1955), pp. 40-58.

3. Hoover, "The General Framework of the Studies," pp. 4-5.

4. *Ibid.*, p. 3.

5. Raymond Vernon, *The Dilemma of Mexico's Development*, p. 88.

6. See Presidencia de la República and Nacional Financiera, *50 años de revolución mexicana en cifras*, p. 115; and American International Investment Corp., *World Currency Charts*, Chart 18 - Mexico, 1963.

Chapter I

THE AGRICULTURAL SECTOR

The Mexican Constitution of 1917 not only created a basic legal and political framework but also provided a program for "social justice" and economic reform. To deal with the problems confronting the country, sweeping powers, limited principally by a prohibition against re-election, were given to the federal government, and in particular, to the President. One of the most economically complex and emotionally loaded issues of that time was the question of how to combat rural poverty. The Constitution placed great emphasis on breaking up the *haciendas* to provide land for the *campesinos*. This program would also have the result of destroying the power of the landed aristocracy who for the most part had supported the Díaz regime.

Land Tenure System

The legal basis for Mexico's present land tenure system rests primarily on Article 27 of the Mexican Constitution of 1917.[1] After declaring that ownership of lands and waters "is vested originally in the Nation"[2] and that there must be indemnification for land appropriated for reason of public utility, Article 27 states:

> The Nation shall at all times have the right to impose on private property such limitations as the public interest may require as well as the right to regulate the enjoyment of natural resources which are susceptible of appropriation, in order to make an equitable distribution of public wealth and to care for its conservation. For this purpose the necessary measures shall be taken for the division of large landed estates; for the development of small agricultural holdings under exploitation; for the creation of new centers of rural population with the lands and waters which may be indispensable to them; for the development of agriculture and for avoiding the destruction of natural resources and the damages which property may suffer to the prejudice of society. The centers of population which lack lands or water or do not possess them in sufficient quantities for the needs of their population shall have the right to be provided with them from the adjoining properties, always having due regard for small agricultural holdings under exploitation.

In regard to communities that lack land, the government was empowered to grant lands and waters sufficient for their needs. No individual unit or area of *dotación*[3] was, however, to be less than ten hectares of irrigated land or its equivalent. Any land expropriated had to be within the immediate vicinity (defined as land within seven kilometers) of the village claiming it and could not impinge upon the inaffectible holdings of a private individual. Currently, the inaffectible holdings or maximum size of privately owned plots may not exceed 100 hectares of irrigated or otherwise choice lands or its equivalent.[4]

The actual administration of the land reform program was entrusted almost exclusively to the executive branch of the government. While the state governors and certain officials within the executive branch of the federal government were to exercise important functions in the land reform process, the President of the Republic was designated as the supreme agrarian authority. An individual whose land was expropriated had neither ordinary legal recourse or access to judicial injunction, unless he had or could obtain a certificate of inaffectibility. While he had the constitutional right to indemnification, he had to petition the government no later than one year from the date the presidential decree expropriating his land was published in the *Diario Oficial*.

For all practical purposes, questions concerning the appropriate land tenure system for Mexico were basically settled by the end of 1940.[5] President Cárdenas firmly established the pattern of dividing large *haciendas* into communally owned lands called *ejidos*[6] and small private holdings. Expropriated lands granted free of charge to a community as an *ejido* could not be mortgaged or sold. In the majority of *ejidos*, the land was distributed to *ejidatarios*, who held their particular plots for life and bequeathed them on their death. When a family left the village, became extinct, or ceased to work a plot, the land reverted to the community. In a few cases, *ejido* land is not subdivided but is worked as a single unit.

Between 1930 and 1940, the *ejido* share of the total land area and of crop land (excluding land owned by the government) rose from 6.3 percent to 22.5 percent and from 13.4 percent to 47.4 percent, respectively.[7] Except for López Mateos and Díaz Ordaz, no President has approached the level of *dotaciones* to *ejidos* recorded during Cárdenas' term. (See Table 1.) The reasons are rather easily discernible. In the first place, there is a limited amount of land that can be distributed, and secondly, *ejidos* have been less efficient as producing units than private agricultural units; "yields per acre on the *ejidos* are in most cases 20 to 25 percent lower."[8]

There are a number of plausible motives that help explain the large spurt in *dotaciones* during the term of López Mateos.[9] By parceling out

Table 1

Dotación of Land to *Ejidos* by Presidential Periods[a]

President	Years in Office	Dotaciones in Hectares
Venustiano Carranza	2- 5-15 to 5-21-20	224,393
Adolfo de la Huerta	5-22-20 to 11-30-20	157,532
Alvaro Obregón	12- 1-20 to 11-30-24	1,677,067
P. Elías Calles	12- 1-24 to 11-30-28	3,195,028
Emilio Portes Gil	12- 1-28 to 2- 4-30	2,065,847
Pascual Ortiz Rubio	2- 5-30 to 9- 1-32	1,203,737
Abelardo Rodríguez	9- 2-32 to 11-30-34	2,094,637
Lázaro Cárdenas	12- 1-34 to 11-30-40	20,072,957
Manuel Avila Camacho	12- 1-40 to 11-30-46	5,327,942
Miguel Alemán	12- 1-46 to 11-30-52	4,057,993
Adolfo Ruiz Cortines	12- 1-52 to 11-30-58	3,664,379
Adolfo López Mateos	12- 1-58 to 11-30-64	16,004,000
Gustavo Díaz Ordaz	12- 1-64 to 11-30-70[b]	23,055,619

[a]The information concerning *dotaciones* in hectars is closely related but does not conform exactly to the time period given. There are several series of figures which differ slightly on *dotaciones* by various periods. Part of the variation stems from calculations based on decrees expropriating land and calculations that attempt to determine the actual amount of land redistributed. Also, some lands have been redistributed more than once.

[b]Figure applies from December 1, 1964, to approximately September 1, 1970.

Sources: Edmundo Flores, *Tratado de economía agrícola*, p. 311. Data concerning distribution by López Mateos were obtained from the Instituto de Investigaciones Agrícolas by José Carral, of the Bank of America. President Díaz Ordaz's September 1, 1970, State of the Union Address.

most of the remaining land available for redistribution, he will undoubtedly be recorded as the President who brought the land reform program to a close and focused attention on the needs for new programs to increase production and improve the peasants' standard of living. Beyond the historical aspect, it served immediate political needs by easing rural discontent and by offering "left-wing" members of Mexico's political elite evidence of his sympathy for at least some of their goals. For the left wing, land distribution has been a "sacred dogma" clothed with revolutionary respectability.

The literature on the agricultural problems of Mexico is replete with arguments over the low productivity of *ejidos* and the measures to be taken to raise productivity.[10] One of the more important restraints on increasing production is that the majority of *ejidos* are subdivided among individual *ejidatarios* into small uneconomic units,[11] militating against the use of machinery and certain modern techniques. The generally low educational attainment of most *ejidatarios*, lack of sufficient moisture for growing crops, overpopulation, and the severe problems involved in financing *ejidos* are other important factors. While these restraints are particularly true for the individually worked *ejidos*, they apply in varying degrees to collectively worked *ejidos* and to privately owned plots.[12]

In spite of the serious handicaps to increasing agricultural output, Mexico has made dramatic gains in agricultural production since 1940.[13] The collectively worked *ejidos*, such as those that specialize in producing cotton and wheat in northern Mexico, henequen in the Yucatan peninsula, or rice in the state of Michoacán, have made effective use of machinery and modern technology.[14] To a large extent, the advances in agricultural production have been achieved because of the collectively worked *ejidos* and the larger privately owned plots.

Although land has been granted to *ejidos* throughout the post-Cárdenas period, it is significant that *ejido* holdings of crop land have declined relative to private holdings. (See Table 2.) Less than 26 percent of the land granted to *ejidos* from 1915 to 1959 was in crop land and only 4 percent constituted irrigated or humid land.[15] The government has also increased the number of privately owned plots by giving farmers who have resided on national lands for more than five years title to the land and by allowing settlers, or colonists, in new centers of population to pay for the land they work over a long period of time. In addition to *dotaciones*, some of the land distributed by President López Mateos resulted in an increased number of private holdings.[16]

In spite of the massive redistribution of land that has occurred since 1917, many peasants are still landless.[17] While President Díaz Ordaz "signed 3,940 resolutions distributing 23,055,619 hectares of land to 372,580 peasants"[18] and had early in his administration pledged himself

The Agricultural Sector

Table 2

Distribution of Nongovernment-Owned Land in Mexico by
Ejidos and Private Owners, and by Land Classification,
1940, 1950, and 1960

(Percentages)

	Privately owned plots		
	Over 5 hectares	5 hectares or less	Ejidos
	1940		
Total Land Area	76.7	0.9	22.5
<u>Crop</u> land	45.4	7.2	47.4
Pasture land	80.9	0.1	19.0
Forest	82.0	–	18.0
Uncultivated productive land	80.6	–	19.4
Agriculturally unproductive land	75.6	–	24.4
	1950		
Total Land Area	72.3	0.9	26.7
<u>Crop</u> land	49.5	6.4	44.1
Pasture land	75.3	0.1	24.5
Forest	77.3	–	22.7
Uncultivated productive land	77.9	–	22.1
Agriculturally unproductive land	77.3	–	22.7
	1960		
Total Land Area	72.9	0.8	26.3
<u>Crop</u> land	51.3	5.3	43.4
Pasture land	75.2	–	24.8
Forest	81.6	–	18.4
Uncultivated productive land	64.7	–	35.3
Agriculturally unproductive land	77.1	0.1	22.8

Sources: Secretaría de Industria y Comercio, Departamento de los Censos, *Censos agropecuarios (1930, 1940, y 1950)*, p. 9, and *Censos agrícola-ganadero y ejidal, 1960, resumen general (1965)*, p. 1.

to redistribute illegal landholdings, he also stressed that small private holdings "are genuine and legitimate creations of the Revolution"[19] and explained that the greater part of the national land offers little promise as sites for new centers of population because they are located in arid or tropical regions. After stating that all Mexicans must contribute to the solution of rural problems, he declared: "To industrialize agricultural production, to create new sources of employment, to strengthen the domestic market in order to enlarge further the centers of manufacturing and create more employment for Mexicans are realizable national goals."[20]

The Agrarian Sector of the Partido Revolucionario Institucional

Mexico is basically a one-party state.[21] The dominant party, Partido Revolucionario Institucional (Institutional Revolutionary Party), which is usually referred to as PRI, infolds virtually every segment of the Mexican population. PRI is composed of three functional interest groups—the Agrarian Sector, the Labor Sector, and the Popular Sector—and is probably the principal mechanism through which these groups interact. It is not always possible to determine the extent to which decisions are made through the PRI and/or established government agencies.

> Because real political power and formal legal authority do not coincide so completely as they do in the United States, access to policy-making is not quite so easy and decisions do not always reflect so satisfactory an evaluation of the relative power positions of the interests involved. But access is possible, and adjustment does take place, so that Mexico has worked out a stable political system.[22]

Thus the PRI is vitally important in that it affords the citizen an opportunity to express his views on present and hoped-for future government action and thereby tends to create a sense of individual participation.

The backbone of the Agrarian Sector is the Confederación Nacional Campesina (National Peasants' Confederation) which was established in 1938 and given legal standing by the government. Theoretically, the Confederación Nacional Campesina represents the *ejidos*[23] in particular and agricultural interests in general. "A few other agricultural interest associations also participate in the sectors' activities, some as integral and permanent parts of the sector and others on a temporary basis."[24] For example, professional agronomists are represented by the Sociedad Agronómica Mexicana, which became an official permanent part of the Agrarian Sector in 1952.

As the basic unit of the Confederación Nacional Campesina is the *ejido,* private farmers have found, or at least believed, that their interests would

The Agricultural Sector

be better served through the Popular Sector of the PRI. Thus the Popular Sector of the PRI includes the Confederación Nacional de la Pequeña Propiedad Agrícola (National Confederation of Small Property Owners) and the Asociación Nacional de Cosecheros (National Association of Harvesters).[25] Laborers who work on farms for wages or are involved in some process of providing services to farmers are frequently represented by a union with membership in the Labor Sector of PRI. In some cases, individuals may be claimed as members of more than one sector of PRI.

Because of its very complexity, the diverse sectors of Mexican agriculture are able to find some organized group within the PRI that attempts, at least in a general way, to promote their economic and social interests. While the power of the Agrarian Sector has reportedly been declining,[26] the present government does appear to be pursuing measures to improve the economic conditions of the rural masses. It is not possible to measure the extent to which this renewed emphasis on agricultural development was brought about through the actions of the Agrarian Sector of the PRI.

Government Intervention in Financing Agricultural Development

In many respects Mexico's economy is still oriented toward agriculture. While the percentage of the labor force actively engaged in agriculture has been declining since 1940, more than half of the labor force has been engaged in agriculture throughout the period, and the absolute number of agricultural workers has risen. (See Table 3.) The share of GNP attributed to agricultural activity has also declined over this period, but more slowly than the labor participation rate. (See Table 4.) The increase in per capita production at a time when labor is shifting to other forms of employment suggests that the marginal productivity per worker is negative or quite low.

While there are reasonably reliable indices of Mexican agricultural production, "their coverage varies widely so that it is impossible to weld them into a consistent series."[27] Estimates for the increase in agricultural production between 1940 and 1960 indicate substantial gains but differ in regard to the rate.[28] While part of the gain is attributable simply to the expansion of land under cultivation,[29] investments in the agricultural sector have also been an important factor.

From 1940 through 1963, the Federal Government, its decentralized agencies, and firms having state participation expended almost 11 percent of the total public fixed investments for agricultural development.[30] (While agricultural investments as a percentage of total public fixed investments reached their lowest levels during the regime of President López Mateos, these investments rose to 12.5 percent of authorized public

Table 3

Occupational Structure of Mexico

	1940	1950	1960	1967
Total Labor Force				
Thousands of persons	5,858.1	8,345.2[a]	11,332.0	14,368.0
Per cent of total	100.0	100.0	100.0	100.0
Agriculture[b]				
Thousands of persons	3,830.9	4,823.9	6,144.9	7,209.0
Per cent of total	65.4	57.8	54.2	50.2
Industry				
Thousands of persons	746.3	1,319.1	2,187.1	3,156.0
Per cent of total	12.7	15.8	19.3	22.0
Commerce and Finance				
Thousands of persons	552.5	684.1	1,074.6	1,509.0
Per cent of total	9.5	8.2	9.5	10.5
Transportation and Communication				
Thousands of persons	149.5	210.6	357.1	536.0
Per cent of total	2.6	2.5	3.1	3.7

Table 3 - Continued

	1940	1950	1960	1967
Services[c]				
Thousands of persons	415.3	879.4	1,525.7	1,958.0
Per cent of total	7.1	10.5	13.5	13.6
Not Specified				
Thousands of persons	163.7	355.0	81.8	
Per cent of total	2.8	4.3	0.4	

[a]Those unemployed thirteen weeks or more are included in the total labor force but not distributed by economic activity.

[b]Includes grazing, forestry, and fishing.

[c]Includes private and government services.

Sources: Secretaría de Industria y Comercio, *Revista de Estadística* (December, 1965) p. 1392, and Nacional Financiera, *Informe anual 1965 and 1967*, pp. 31 and 54, respectively.

Table 4

Distribution of Gross National Product by
Type of Economic Activity, 1940-69

(Percentages)

	1940	1950	1960	1969[c]
Agriculture[a]	20.5	23.8	20.4	11.3
Industry	24.9	32.5	37.2	33.5
Mining	4.4	3.2	2.2	1.4
Petroleum	1.7	2.9	4.5	3.4
Manufacturing	16.4	22.2	25.6	22.1
Construction	1.8	3.3	3.5	5.1
Electric power	.6	.9	1.3	1.5
Transportation and Communication	5.8	5.1	5.3	2.7
Commerce	26.4	22.7	20.9	29.9
Others[b]	22.4	15.9	16.3	22.5

[a] Includes grazing, forestry, and fishing.

[b] Private and government services.

[c] Figures for 1969 are adjusted for bank services.

Sources: Banco Nacional de Comercio Exterior, *Mexico, 1960: Facts, Figures, and Trends*, p. 101; and Banco de México, *Informe anual 1961* and *1969*, pp. 27 and 58-61, respectively.

investments for 1970.)[31] Greatest emphasis has traditionally been on the construction of irrigation projects, especially large irrigation projects. In fact, investments in irrigation accounted for 92 percent of total public investments in agriculture, and investments for large irrigation projects constituted 88 percent of the investments in irrigation.[32] The need for irrigation has been established by various government studies. Virtually, all of Mexico's land area suffers from a deficiency of rainfall, a sufficient quantity of rainfall but at very irregular or unpredictable frequency, or an oversupply of moisture. "Only about 1 percent of the total land area would not need irrigation at some time of the year to ensure consistently high agricultural production."[33]

While President Lázaro Cárdenas attempted to direct irrigation expenditures primarily for the well being of *ejidatarios,* his successors appeared to be most concerned with increasing agricultural production. Investments in irrigation have obviously contributed to the general increase in Mexican agricultural production and to the disparity between production on private agricultural plots and *ejidos.* The total land area benefited by government irrigation projects expanded nearly twelvefold from 1940 to 1964,[34] and 55 percent of this area represented land that had not been cultivated before. Production per hectare of irrigated land, as would be expected, has been substantially higher, and the value of harvests has been less subject to fluctuations.[35]

In 1958, the *ejidatarios'* holdings constituted 42 percent of the total land area of the irrigation districts operated by the Secretaría de Recursos Hidráulicos (Ministry of Hydraulic Resources). Among the 193,879 *ejidatarios,* 84 percent had plots under five hectares; 13 percent had plots from five to twenty hectares; and the remaining 3 percent had plots over twenty but under fifty hectares. Among holdings of private owners and colonists, 51 percent were under five hectares; 30 percent were from five to twenty hectares; 12 percent were from twenty to fifty hectares; and 7 percent were over fifty hectares. As the per-hectare value of harvests of land within irrigation districts in 1958 was placed at 2,266 pesos, a holder of less than five hectares would have been able to anticipate a return on his production of something under 11,330 pesos or $906, and 74 percent of the holders of irrigated land had less than five hectares. The average return on five hectares of nonirrigated land in 1958, however, was only 4,355 pesos or $348. From these figures, it is not difficult to understand why the average peasant—even a peasant who is fortunate enough to hold irrigated land—does not invest to any significant degree in machinery, fertilizer, or improved seeds.

While the government has invested heavily in irrigation projects, it has not appropriated sufficient funds for repair, maintenance, or construction of auxiliary works. One consequence of this neglect was the need for

Table 5

Gross Public Fixed Investment[a] for Agricultural Development, 1940-70

(Millions of Pesos)

	Total Agricultural Investments	Total	Irrigation Large Projects	Irrigation Small Projects	Other	Livestock	Forestry	Agricultural Investments as a Percentage of Total Investment[b]
1940	44	36	36	—	8			15.2
1941	59	57	54	3	2			17.5
1942	65	63	58	5	2			14.0
1943	86	83	75	8	3			15.1
1944	122	117	105	12	5			18.6
1945	144	140	126	14	4			17.0
1946	193	189	169	20	4			19.3
1947	258	228	213	15	5	25		19.7
1948	319	249	234	15	10	60		20.7
1949	458	260	241	19	4	194		23.4
1950	515	372	353	19	9	134		19.3
1951	579	502	468	34	11	66		20.4
1952	561	548	482	66	13			17.1

Table 5 - Continued

	Total Agricultural Investments	Total	Irrigation Large Projects	Irrigation Small Projects	Other	Live-stock	Forestry	Agricultural Investments as a Percentage of Total Investment[b]
1953	563	506	444	62	57			18.3
1954	626	604	534	70	22			15.0
1955	605	602	533	69	3			13.7
1956	649	588	535	53	60	1		14.2
1957	670	641	542	99	27	2		11.9
1958	698	644	487	157	47	5	2	11.3
1959	752	738	638	100	10	2	1	11.5
1960	580	567	480	87	10	2	1	6.9
1961	953	924	812	112	19	2	8	9.2
1962	818	773	665	108	40	1	4	7.6
1963	1,415	1,376	1,244	132	36	2	1	10.2
1964	2,170	2,036	1,895	141	131	2	1	12.5

Table 5 - Continued

Year	Total Agricultural Investments[c]	Agricultural Investments as a Percentage of Total Investments
1965	1,548	9.5
1966	1,927	9.3
1967	2,327	10.6
1968	2,940	12.0
1969	3,605	13.1
1970	4,000	13.2

[a]Public investments comprise the investments of the federal government, its decentralized agencies, and firms having state participation.

[b]See Table 25, Chapter IV, for figures showing total public investments.

[c]Data for 1965-70 not available on same breakdown as prior years.

Source: Secretaría de la Presidencia, Dirección de Inversiones Públicas, *México: Inversión pública federal, 1925-1963*, pp. 43-6 and 119, and *México: Inversión pública federal, 1965-1970*, pp. 136-137 and 209.

Table 6

Accumulated Land Area Benefited by
Government Irrigation Projects, 1940-68[a]

(In Hectares)

	Cumulative Total	New Lands Opened for Cultivation	Land Previously Cultivated
1940	267,095	147,366	119,729
1946	816,224	419,867	396,357
1952	1,441,736	806,535	635,201
1958	2,189,527	1,357,693	831,834
1964	2,440,294	1,506,823	933,471
1968	2,698,690	1,719,636	979,054

[a]Accumulation of hectares since 1926.

Source: Nacional Financiera, *Nacional Financiera en el desarrollo económico de México, 1934-64*, p. 20, and *Informe anual, 1968*, p. 63.

"rehabilitation of 22 large irrigation districts where inadequate drainage systems have led to rising water tables and consequently to deterioration of soils."[36] The potential production gains from irrigation projects have also been limited because public "expenditures for the promotion of improved agricultural methods, for research and extension services, and for the protection and improvement of natural resources were conspicuously low."[37] The national agricultural credit banks have as one of their functions promoted the adoption of modern agricultural methods and equipment, but Mexico's agricultural extension service has been functioning only since 1953.[38]

Since 1941, the Rockefeller Foundation has assisted in various programs to expand agricultural production in Mexico.[39] One of its earliest and most important activities was in supporting research aimed at increasing the output of the country's basic food crops, particularly corn and wheat.[40] The establishment of a national corn commission in 1947 was an outgrowth of Foundation efforts, started in 1943, to improve corn cultivation.[41] The Foundation has also engaged in campaigns against crop and animal diseases as well as in public health programs. The striking gains in wheat production that have been recorded since 1946 were, to an important degree, made possible through the work of the Rockefeller Foundation. A number of Mexicans have become agricultural or public health specialists as a result of training programs or study grants provided by the Foundation.

In a 1966 Rockefeller Foundation report, it was stated: "Because of the tremendous advances that Mexico has made in the production of its basic food crops, the Foundation has shifted emphasis in this country to the production of materials and information more broadly useful in the improvement of food supplies through the tropics and semitropics."[42]

Reliable data on private investment in agriculture during recent years are not readily available. Figures that do exist indicate that private investment in agriculture was 13 percent greater than public investment from 1940 through 1950.[43] If González Santos' figures for private investment in agriculture during 1954 and 1955 are accurate, private investment during that two-year period would have exceeded public investment by about 150 percent.[44] This figure does not appear to be unreasonable considering that President Miguel Alemán had a constitutional amendment enacted in 1946 that permitted individuals to hold up to 300 hectares of irrigated land for the cultivation of certain crops and that his regime reputedly encouraged certain families to amass substantial landholdings.[45]

The Mexican Government has also attempted—sometimes in a very half-hearted manner—to stimulate agricultural development and raise the standard of living for the rural masses through the creation of various national agricultural credit institutions. Of the important national agricultural credit banks, the Banco Nacional de Crédito Agrícola, established in 1926, was designed to assist agricultural development through loans, technical assistance, and other services to the poorest peasants. At the present time, the Banco Nacional de Crédito Agrícola is also engaged in various processing and marketing operations. The Banco Nacional de Crédito Ejidal came into being in 1935 in order to promote the well being of the *ejidatarios*. Actually, the Banco Nacional de Crédito Agrícola was split into two in 1935 because some influential persons believed that credits to *ejidatarios* were being neglected. After the split, the Banco Nacional de Crédito Agrícola directed its efforts toward improving the status of private farmers. In 1940, the Banco Nacional de Crédito Agrícola and the Banco Nacional de Crédito Ejidal extended 6.3 million pesos[46] and 65.6 million pesos[47] in loans, respectively, compared with 526.4 million pesos[48] and 1,249.5 million pesos[49] in 1960.

The Banco Nacional de Comercio Exterior, founded in 1937, has been concerned with various aspects of agricultural development because of its role as Mexico's principal foreign trade bank. According to the reports of the Banco Nacional de Comercio Exterior, a sizable portion of the total credits they extend are for production, and mainly agricultural production.[50] In 1946, production loans accounted for 141.1 million pesos out of a total of 653.8 million pesos.[51] In 1960 and 1964, total loans were 3,484.0 million pesos and 2,904.4 million pesos, respectively, and production loans for the same years were 976.1 million pesos and 1,889.1 million pesos.[52]

In 1960, slightly over 80 percent of the funds for production loans of the Banco Nacional de Comercio Exterior were obtained and managed by the Nacional Crédito Agrícola and Crédito Ejidal banks. In 1964, 85 percent of the production loans were handled by these two national agrarian development banks, with Crédito Agrícola accounting for 70 percent of the 1,618.8 million pesos.[53] Traditionally, the production loans of these banks have been directed toward financing cotton, maize, wheat, rice, and several other crops.

The relationship among these three banks is quite important as they have been organized in such a manner as to assure that the program and wishes of the President have a definite impact on their actions.[54] Thus, these banks through their credit policies provide important support for other government programs, such as measures to regulate prices. Prior to 1961, for example, a sizable portion of the credits extended by the Banco Nacional de Comercio Exterior were destined for price regulation, and for the most part, were utilized by the Compañía Exportadora e Importadora

(CEIMSA) or the Nacional Distribuidora y Reguladora.

Since 1940 (and even before that), there has been a continuing discussion of the need for more agricultural credit, as well as complaints that the two national agrarian development banks have made loans primarily to the well-to-do farmers. Some, however, have argued that these banks have been too lax in their loan standards. These conflicting charges emanate from the fact that, "the agricultural development banks were charged with the extension of credit to the traditionally submarginal, 'economically irresponsible' sector of agriculture."[55]

The government has considerable power to influence the flow of both private and public credits to various sectors of the economy.[56] As would be expected, the percentage of total financing extended by the banking system to agricultural (including livestock) production has varied from one presidential period to another. (See Table 7.) Credits for agricultural production declined sharply during the last two years of President Ávila Camacho's term and accounted for less than 12 percent of the total credits extended during the Alemán administration. Ávila Camacho was particularly concerned with promoting industrialization, and World War II provided Mexico with a unique opportunity to industrialize. "Alemán proceeded upon the principle which Ávila Camacho himself had seemed more and more disposed to adopt—the principle that what was good for Mexican business was probably good for Mexico."[57] President Ruiz Cortines, however, placed considerably more emphasis on agricultural development and the social needs of the peasants, and this concern is reflected in the higher percentage of credit channeled to agricultural development. The percentage of banking system credits as well as public investments to agriculture were relatively low during the term of President López Mateos, who received considerable publicity as a champion of the rural sector because of his program of land distribution. Theoretically, the actions taken during his administration could be interpreted as one answer to the question: "How can peasants be encouraged to produce a cumulative surplus of food and fibers over and above their own consumption, and how can this surplus largely be channeled to investment activity in the nonfarm sector without requiring in exchange an equivalent transfer of productive value to the farm sector?"[58]

Statements by President Díaz Ordaz and various high-ranking officials in his administration consistently indicated the intention of directing more resources to the agricultural sector. In March, 1965, it was announced that the President ordered "the creation of the Banco Nacional Agropecuario [National Agriculture and Livestock Bank], with initial capital of 1,500 million pesos and with the character of a national credit institution."[59] This bank, which operates throughout the Republic, was

Table 7

Financing by Mexican Credit Institutions
for Agricultural Production,[a] 1942-69

	Total Financing (millions of pesos)	Financing for Agricultural Production[b] (millions of pesos)	Agricultural Financing as a Percentage of Total Financing
1940	n.a.	n.a.	n.a.
1941	n.a.	n.a.	n.a.
1942	2,024.2	247.9	21.1
1943	2,529.6	528.5	20.9
1944	3,249.9	725.6	22.3
1945	4,075.7	583.6	14.3
1946	4,908.4	588.4	12.0
1947	5,748.9	703.0	12.2
1948	7,040.8	771.3	11.0
1949	8,172.0	903.3	11.1
1950	8,972.7	1,059.9	11.8
1951	10,767.3	1,230.0	11.4
1952	11,887.5	1,507.1	12.7
1953	13,497.8	2,015.8	14.9
1954	16,811.4	2,103.5	12.5
1955	17,672.7	2,786.7	15.8
1956	19,657.6	3,277.3	16.7
1957	22,464.0	3,561.4	15.9
1958	26,583.3	3,998.8	15.0

Table 7 - Continued

	Total Financing (millions of pesos)	Financing for Agricultural Production[b] (millions of pesos)	Agricultural Financing as a Percentage of Total Financing
1959	31,269.0	4,738.5	15.2
1960	39,780.5	5,811.9	14.6
1961	46,055.9	6,582.8	14.3
1962	53,454.4	7,360.7	13.8
1963	61,251.5	8,237.0	13.4
1964	74,434.9	9,317.9	12.5
1965	87,374.0	10,635.3	12.2
1966	104,629.5	12,688.8	12.1
1967	121,105.3	14,025.6	11.6
1968	138,767.6	15,355.9	11.1
1969	167,224.9	16,188.0	9.7

[a] Does not include insurance companies.

[b] Includes credits for livestock production.

Source: Banco de México, *Informe anual 1965* and *1969*, pp. 107 and 102, respectively.

designed to supplement existing credit facilities available to *ejidatarios* and small private farmers by operating as a "bankers' bank" to these institutions and by establishing new credit institutions where needed in areas favorable to agricultural development. The Fondo de Garantía y Fomento para la Agricultura, Ganadería y Avicultura (Fund for the Guarantee and Development of Agriculture, Grazing, and Poultry), a fiduciary for the Banco de México, and the Banco Nacional Agropecuario work together as a single system. Furthermore, Rodrigo Gómez, the late Director General of the Banco de México told the twenty-second convention of the Asociación de Banqueros de México: "Limited public resources require that an increasing proportion of the funds of private credit institutions be used for agricultural development."[60] In spite of all these statements, credit extended by the Mexican financial system for agricultural production continued to decline as a percentage of the total through 1969.

Government Intervention in the Pricing and Marketing Process

The Mexican Government has a long history of directly intervening in the pricing and marketing of agricultural commodities. Two approaches have been utilized in government attempts to regulate prices. In both cases the influence of the executive branch of the federal government has been paramount. One method used in efforts to regulate prices has been to influence the supply and distribution of particular articles, and the other has been to establish a maximum price for various commodities by administrative decree. Article 28 of the Constitution of 1917 provided the first legal basis for price regulation by stating: "The Law shall severely castigate, and the authorities shall efficaciously prosecute, every concentration or cornering (*acaparamiento*) in a few hands of articles of necessary consumption for the purpose of obtaining a price rise."[61]

A series of agencies were established to administer government programs aimed at regulating the supply and distribution of certain commodities. The Comité Regulador del Mercado del Trigo (Committee to Regulate the Wheat Market) was founded in 1937. This was replaced in 1938 by the Comité Regulador del Mercado de las Subsistencias (Committee to Regulate the Market for Subsistence Commodities) and in 1941 by the Nacional Distribuidora y Reguladora. In 1943 the last-named was joined by the Banco Nacional de Crédito Agrícola, the Banco Nacional de Crédito Ejidal, la Compañía Exportadora e Importadora Mexicana (CEIMSA), and the Comité de Aforos (Commodity Appraisal Committee) to form a consortium. In 1950, CEIMSA became the regulating agency.[62] In early 1961, the Compañía Nacional de Subsistencias Populares (CONASUPO—National Committee for Popular

Subsistence Commodities) legally replaced CEIMSA, but "in another sense, they deserve separate identities, since the traditional functions of CEIMSA persist under the old organizational framework and the name of CEIMSA, while new merchandising is promoted as CONASUPO operations."[63] According to the chief officer of CONASUPO, its ultimate responsibility is "to protect the *ejidatarios* and the peasants with small plots of land by means of minimum guaranteed prices, and to provide provisions of the best quality and at the lowest price to the poorer segments of the population."[64]

Meaningful official statistical information detailing the activities of this series of agencies is not readily available. In the 1940s and early 1950s the government was accused of creating monopolies in the trade of certain commodities. It has been reported that in 1942 the government had a monopoly in the foreign and domestic trade of maize, beans, and rice.[65] President Ruiz Cortines in a message on May 14, 1954, declared that a free market in maize was re-established and that CEIMSA would in the future operate only on a marginal basis.[66] From 1953 to 1958, CEIMSA reputedly purchased 8 million metric tons of maize, beans, and wheat which was estimated to have been approximately 25 percent of the total national consumption of these commodities.[67] If these figures are reasonably accurate, CEIMSA would have enjoyed a substantial marginal influence. During the 1954-58 period, price increases, as reflected in the Cost of Foodstuffs Index in Mexico City, were more moderate than during the presidential terms of either Ávila Camacho or Alemán. (See Table 8.) While a heavy volume of maize imports[68] contributed to the slower rate of advance in food prices, production increases in certain basic commodities were also greater than in the two previous presidential periods. (See Table 9.) In addition, Fernández and Acosta state that the government gave CEIMSA subsidies approximating 1,412 million pesos during this five-year period.[69]

During the term of President López Mateos, emphasis was placed on making Mexico self-sufficient in foodstuffs and a net exporter, rather than importer, of maize, wheat, and other commodities. Production was stimulated by the establishment of relatively high guaranteed prices, and surpluses were disposed of through exportation by CEIMSA. At the same time, domestic food prices were considered to be high for the poorer segments of the population. The government through Compañía Distribuidora de Subsistencias Populares (Company to Distribute Popular Subsistence Commodities), a filial enterprise of CONASUPO, expanded its network of retail outlets which sold basic commodities at quite low prices. Two other filial enterprises, the Compañía Rehidratadora de Leche (Milk Dehydration and Reconstitution Company) and Compañía Maíz

Table 8

Cost of Foodstuffs Index in Mexico City
Sixteen Articles at Retail Price

(Base: 1954=100)

Year	Index	Year	Index
1940	20.8	1955	118.0
1941	21.8	1956	122.9
1942	23.7	1957	129.3
1943	31.6	1958	142.9
1944	45.4	1959	147.8
1945	50.8	1960	151.7
1946	60.2	1961	157.1
1947	61.3	1962	157.2
1948	61.7	1963	156.6
1949	64.6	1964	163.8
1950	70.5	1965	166.5
1951	90.0	1966	172.8
1952	99.5	1967	177.2
1953	93.2	1968	182.8
1954	100.0	1969	185.5

Sources: Banco Nacional de Comercio Exterior, *México*, *1960*, p. 106, and Banco de México, *Informe anual*, 1964 and 1969, pp. 84 and 74, respectively.

Table 9

Production of Maize, Wheat, and Beans in Mexico, 1940-67

(Thousands of metric tons)

Year	Maize	Wheat	Beans
1940	1,640	464	97
1941	2,124	434	160
1942	2,363	489	183
1943	1,808	364	157
1944	2,316	374	183
1945	2,186	347	162
1946	2,383	340	139
1947	2,518	422	199
1948	2,832	477	210
1949	2,871	503	231
1950	3,122	587	250
1951	3,424	590	240
1952	3,202	512	244
1953	3,722	671	299
1954	4,488	839	399
1955	4,490	850	449
1956	4,382	1,243	432
1957	4,500	1,377	410
1958	5,277	1,337	510
1959	5,563	1,266	581
1960	5,386	1,190	723
1961	6,246	1,401	723
1962	6,338	1,455	666
1963	6,870	1,703	677
1964	8,454	1,527	892
1965	8,678	1,609	358
1966	9,038	1,612	1,002
1967	8,975	2,058	1,008

Sources: Nacional Financiera, *50 años de revolución mexicana en cifras*, pp. 54-55, and Nacional Financiera, *Informe 1964* and *1967*, pp. 156 and 91, respectively.

Industrializado (Maize Commission), were charged with maintaining some balance between the desired quality and cost of production of milk and maize and a low retail price.

The government's involvement in regulating agricultural prices has been complicated by the number of publicly espoused government goals. There has been a desire to achieve self-sufficiency in agricultural production,[70] to encourage the cultivation of export crops to earn badly needed foreign exchange, to maintain relatively low food prices for the low income urban dwellers, and to raise the living standards of the rural masses. It is understandable that measures taken to cope with these diverse and frequently inconsistent objectives—particularly when the priority of goals has been subject to change because of shifting world conditions—have been characterized as lacking orientation, contradictory, or self-defeating. It is obvious, however, that the government through various agencies under the control of the executive branch exercises substantial influence in the supply and distribution of certain agricultural commodities. Interestingly, however, "there are no direct subsidies on either acreage or production in Mexico."[71]

Regulating agricultural prices by influencing the supply and distribution of commodities has not only led to restricting "imports through high duties and a strict licensing system"[72] but also to building warehouses throughout the Republic. Almacenes Nacionales de Depósito was established in 1936. At the end of 1940, its paid-in capital amounted to 4.2 million pesos.[73] It rose to 172.5 million pesos by the end of 1964.[74] In a speech President Díaz Ordaz stated: "Almacenes Nacionales de Depósito currently have 818 of their own and 613 rented warehouses with a capacity of 4 million metric tons."[75] In his last state of the union address, he said, "From 1965 to 1970, Almacenes Nacionales de Depósito invested 459 million pesos in silos, warehouses, port facilities, machinery and storage equipment."[76]

In 1950, Congress enacted the law entitled *Atribuciones del Ejecutivo en Materia Económica* (Powers of the President in Economic Matters). This law broadened the scope of government price regulation from articles of necessary consumption to foodstuffs for general consumption, and allowed the government to set prices by decree.[77] An indication of the sweeping nature of this law is clear from the following quotation: "The President is given power not only to determine by decree the merchandise and distribution of which shall be controlled by the Government but also he is granted power to determine wholesale and retail prices, with due consideration for a reasonable profit . . ."[78]

The Dirección General de Precios (Bureau of Prices), under the Secretaría de Economía (which was later renamed Secretaría de Industria y Comercio), was created on March 28, 1951, to implement this law. The *Memoria* of the Secretaría de Economía that covered the period from September, 1950, to August, 1951, reported that the Dirección General de Precios was working with five special committees dealing with the pricing or distribution of agricultural products and had "levied 698 fines [totaling 98,750 pesos] against merchants in the Federal District who had not respected the prices officially fixed by the Secretaría de Economía."[79] During 1957, there were fifty-four foodstuffs and articles of general use for which a fixed price has been established.[80] In June, 1965, the Secretaría de Industria y Comercio had established maximum retail and wholesale prices for forty-eight articles of necessary consumption (not all of which were agricultural) and had begun studies to determine whether or not to fix prices for fish and meat.[81]

In discussing price regulation, several factors must be stressed. Here is another example where considerable power to intervene in the economy of the country has been placed in the hands of the President and as a consequence to those responsible to him. Also, in Vernon's terms, "the distinction between form and substance needs to be emphasized . . ."[82] When the government "could not retain the substance of a measure to protect the urban poor, [it] still tried valiantly to maintain the form."[83] Because of this attitude, price regulations have not been uniformly enforced. Considerable influence rests with the official who is able to decide whether or not to set a maximum price on a particular article and whether or not to punish violations of a particular regulation.

Summary

The Mexican Government, operating within the constitutional framework, has been deeply involved in the agricultural sector of the economy and, in turn, has attempted to engage the rural community in the nation's political dialogue through the Agrarian Sector of the PRI. While agricultural production has recorded substantial gains since 1940, rural poverty remains a pressing problem. The government's land reform program has destroyed the *hacienda* as a viable institution, but many peasants now live in poverty attributed to the *minifundio*. As the amount of arable land available for redistribution under the existing land reform program has been virtually exhausted, Mexico must find new economic and political answers to its rural problems.[84]

Economic programs must be carried out within a socio-political context. The *ejido* system has not proven to be the most efficient producing unit, but it has undoubtedly contributed to the political stability of the country. Perhaps the greatest virtue of the small inefficient individually worked *ejido* plot is that it has provided employment to

The Agricultural Sector

many Mexicans who would otherwise be unable to find jobs. According to the agricultural census of 1960, the percentage of total land and crop land held by *ejidos* declined modestly from levels prevailing in 1950.

The Díaz Ordaz administration indicated that it would direct a greater share of the country's fixed investments and financial credits to the rural sector. This goal was not accomplished.

Now President Luis Echeverría Álvarez has proclaimed improvement in the agricultural sector to be a prime target of his administration. The success of his program remains to be seen. In the past, the major portion of fixed public investments for agricultural development has been for irrigation facilities. Of course, the supply of water, and thereby the potential for irrigation projects, is limited, but investments are needed to capitalize fully on the potentials of existing irrigation complexes. Beyond this, the need for more agricultural research, extension services, and rural education is quite obvious.

The government has committed itself to maintain price controls over certain commodities of necessary consumption. Mexico's slim margin of gold and foreign exchange will continue to be a factor in decisions concerning crops to be grown—or crops for which financing will be available—and the extent to which the goal of agricultural self-sufficiency will be abridged.

President Echeverría has undertaken the task of reforming and strengthening the *ejido* system and the position of small landowners through the Agrarian Reform Act which came into force on May 1, 1971. Basically, the Reform Act attempts to simplify and decentralize various agricultural administrative procedures, to provide for secret ballots and restrict possibilities for reelection of *ejido* authorities, and to stimulate production through increased credit, advanced technology, and changed organizational forms.

Notes

1. Most of the procedures to implement the agrarian reform program were spelled out in a series of agrarian codes promulgated between 1934 and 1942.

2. All quotations from the Mexican Constitution of 1917 are, unless otherwise specified, taken from Joseph Wheless, *Compendium of the Laws of Mexico*. This and the following constitutional quotation are found on pp. 595 and 595-96, respectively.

3. There is no exact equivalent for this word in the English language; it refers to a grant of land at no charge to a center of population. There are, however, a number of regulations that specify the legal nature and restrictions on land obtained through the land reform program.

4. One hectare of irrigated or otherwise choice land is equivalent to two hectares of temporal rainfall land, four hectares of relative drought land, and eight hectares of arid mountainous land. Special regulations are followed in regard to land used for raising livestock. Furthermore, there are exemptions if certain crops are raised. For example, the maximum plot legally permissible is 150 hectares for cultivating cotton and 300 hectares for growing bananas, sugar cane, coffee, henequen, and certain other perennial crops.

5. For a discussion of attempts by various officials to distribute land primarily on the basis of private ownership, see Raymond G. Conatser, "Land Reform and Economic Development: Mexico 1930-1960," pp. 32-53.

6. The word *ejido* refers to the land area owned in common by a center of population and utilized for agricultural production. It is a relic from the Indian landholding system that had virtually disappeared by 1917. The *ejido* system was re-created in modern Mexico.

7. Computed from Secretaría de Industria y Comercio, Departamento de los Censos, *Censos agropecuarios* (1930, 1940, and 1950), p. 9.

8. U. S. Department of Agriculture, Foreign Agricultural Service, *Land Distribution in Mexico*, p. 10.

9. See p. 18 for another possible motive.

10. See Lucio Mendieta y Núñez, *El problema agrario de México*; Edmundo Flores, *Tratado de economía agrícola*; Ramón Fernández y Fernández, *Economía agrícola y reforma agraria*; Armando González Santos, *La agricultura: Estructura y utilización de los recursos*; Manuel Moreno Sánchez et al., *Política ejidal*; Moisés González Navarro, "Mexico: The Lop-sided Revolution," in *Obstacles to Change in Latin America*; Juan Rodríguez Mannch," Los ejidatarios, los comisariados ejidales y el crédito," *Estudios Agrarios* 2 (January-April, 1962), pp. 27-37.

11. Using available government statistics, one writer calculated that the average *ejidatario* had only six hectares of crop land. See Edmund K. Faltermayer, "We're Bullish on Mexico," *Fortune* 72 (September, 1965), p. 254. Edmundo Flores places the average *ejidatario*'s plot at around twenty-three hectares; this figure, however, includes all types of land, not just crop land. See "Dinámica del desarrollo agrícola de México," *Comercio Exterior* 15 (October, 1965), p. 713.

12. Comisión Nacional de los Salarios Mínimos, *Memoria de los trabajos de 1963* (1964), p. xxi.

13. See below under "Government Intervention in Financing Agricultural Development."

14. For a brief discussion of collectively worked *ejidos*, see Conatser, pp. 56-59.

15. U. S. Department of Agriculture, *Land Distribution in Mexico*, p. 7.

16. *Ibid.*, p. 8. Also, interview with G. Xavier Guajardo, Banco de Londres y México.

17. Paul P. Kennedy, "Rural Mexicans Warned on Land: Presidential Candidate Says Acreage Grants Near End," *New York Times*, June 14, 1964, p. 7. Also, Henry Giniger, "Many in Mexican Rural Area Are Still Hungering for Land," *New York Times*, June 9, 1966, p. 14.

18. *The News* (Mexico City), September 2, 1969, p. 66.

19. Gustavo Díaz Ordaz, "Aspectos económicos del informe presidencial," as printed in *Comercio Exterior* 15 (September, 1965), p. 625.

20. *Ibid.*

21. There are a number of works that deal with Mexico's political system and political parties. In particular, see Frank R. Brandenburg, "Mexico: An Experiment in One-Party Democracy"; William P. Tucker, *The Mexican Government Today;* George I. Blanksten, "The Politics of Latin America" in *The Politics of the Developing Areas*; and Robert E. Scott, *Mexican Government in Transition*.

22. Scott, p. 23.

23. *Ibid.*, p. 162. Scott reported that two and a half million *ejidatarios* were considered as members of the Confederación Nacional Campesina.

24. *Ibid.*, p. 163.

25. *Ibid.*, p. 167. Scott reports that 865,000 small farm proprietors were represented by these two organizations.

26. See Scott, pp. 170-72, and Tucker, p. 54.

27. Richard W. Parks, "The Role of Agriculture in Mexican Economic Development," *Inter-American Economic Affairs* 18 (Summer, 1964), p. 4. In Presidencia de la República and Nacional Financiera, *50 años de revolución mexicana en cifras*, p. 52, there is an index using 1900 as the base year that records the volume of agricultural production in 1940 and 1960 as 134.9 and 429.5, respectively.

28. Paul Lamartine Yates, *El desarrollo regional de México*, p. 54. Also, Parks, p. 6.

29. According to the agricultural census of 1940 and 1960, crop land rose from almost 15 million hectares to nearly 24 million hectares.

30. Computed from: Secretaría de la Presidencia, Dirección de Inversiones Públicas, *México: Inversión pública federal, 1925-63*, pp. 43-46 and 119.

31. See Table 5.

32. *México: Inversión pública federal, 1925-63*, pp. 43-46 and 119.

33. Walter Thompson de México, *The Mexican Market*, p. 77.

34. An additional 1,200,000 hectares of land are irrigated by special commissions created to develop larger hydrographic basins. See *Mexico: 1963*, prepared by Banco Nacional de Comercio Exterior (translated by Mildred Russell), p. 219. Frank R. Brandenburg in *The Making of Modern Mexico*, p. 259, estimates that 1,775,000 hectares are irrigated through private facilities. See Table 6.

35. This sentence and the following paragraph are based on computations made from tables appearing in Adolfo Orive Alba, *La política de irrigación en México*, pp. 203, 214, and 215.

36. U. S. Department of Agriculture, "More Irrigated Land for Mexico's Crops," *Foreign Agriculture* (November 11, 1963), p. 6.

37. International Bank for Reconstruction and Development, Combined Mexican Working Party, *The Economic Development of Mexico*, p. 22.

38. Katherine E. Rice, *Basic Data on the Economy of Mexico*, p. 7.

39. Tucker, *Mexican Government Today*, p. 291.

40. See Jacob G. Harrar, *Mexican Agricultural Program*. On p. 22 the author states, "The heart of the research program for the present is corn improvement."

41. Combined Mexican Working Party, *Economic Development of Mexico*, p. 29.

42. *Programs in Agricultural Sciences: Annual Report 1964-1965*, p. 14.

43. Combined Mexican Working Party, *Economic Development of Mexico*, p. 206.

44. Armando González Santos, "La agricultura y utilización de los recursos — México, 1957," as cited in Rice, *Basic Data on the Economy of Mexico*, p. 7.

45. Brandenburg, *Making of Modern Mexico*, p. 106, discusses the Alemán period in the following terms: "Inasmuch as the minimum size of agricultural property was to be not less than ten *hectáreas* (24.7 acres) of irrigated land or its equivalent, land was allotted under two sets of standards: about 25 acres for a peon, and up to 741 acres for Alemán's friends."

46. Ernest Moore, *Evolución de las instituciones financieras en México*, p. 144.

47. *Ibid.*, p. 151.

48. *Ibid.*, p. 311.

49. *Ibid.*, p. 314.

50. Banco Nacional de Comercio Exterior, *Informe, 1964*, p. 53, states: "It is well known that the dominant type of credit operations are destined for agricultural production."

51. Moore, p. 321.

52. Banco Nacional de Comercio Exterior, *Informe, 1961*, p. 38, and *Informe, 1964*, p. 41.

53. *Ibid.*, p. 53.

54. See William P. Glade and Charles W. Anderson, *The Political Economy of Mexico*, pp. 137-43.

55. *Ibid.*, p. 147.

56. See Chapter III, pp. 68-71.

57. Vernon, *Dilemma of Mexico's Development*, p. 101.

58. Wyn F. Owen, "The Double Development Squeeze on Agriculture," *American Economic Review* 56 (March, 1966), p. 43.

59. "Creación del Banco Nacional Agropecuario," *El Mercado de Valores* (March 8, 1965), p. 137.

60. Rodrigo Gómez, "El desarrollo del sistema financiero," reprinted in *El Mercado de Valores* (March 28, 1966), p. 309.

61. Wheless, *Compendium of the Laws of Mexico*, p. 28.

62. Ramón Fernández y Fernández and Ricardo Acosta, *Política agrícola*, pp. 200-01.

63. Brandenburg, *Making of Modern Mexico*, p. 315.

64. "Las subsistencias populares y los precios de garantía," *Comercio Exterior* 15 (October, 1965), p. 725.

65. Fernández y Fernández and Acosta, *Política agrícola*, p. 201, cite a speech by César Martino, "El Banco Nacional de Crédito Agrícola: Nota sobre sus antecedentes y funcionamiento actual," given at the Second Inter-American Conference on Agriculture in 1942.

66. *Ibid.*, p. 206.

67. *Ibid.*, p. 213.

68. Marco Antonio Durán, "Perspectivas de la producción y del comercio del trigo y del maíz," *Comercio Exterior* 16 (March, 1966), p. 176.

69. Fernández y Fernández and Acosta, *Política agrícola*, p. 214.

70. President Díaz Ordaz in his first *Informe presidencial* stated that no country can hope to be self-sufficient and that it would be better to import grain from abroad if it would save the country money, p. 626.

71. U. S. Department of Agriculture, *Agricultural Policies of Foreign Governments*. Agricultural Handbook no. 132, Economic Research Service, rev. March, 1964, p.18.

72. *Ibid.*, p. 17.

73. Moore, *Evolución de las instituciones financieras en México*, p. 152.

74. Asociación de Banqueros de México, *Anuario financiero de México*, 1964, p. 144.

75. P. 626 of his first *Informe presidencial*.

76. P. 5b from *The News* (Mexico City), September 2, 1970.

77. See pp. 40-41 for other aspects of this law.

78. Pan American Union, *Laws of Mexico: In Matters Affecting Business* (Washington, D.C.: 1956), p. 160.

79. Pp. 167-68.

80. Secretaría de Economía, *Memoria 1957*, p. 341.

81. Octaviano Campos Salas in a speech delivered on June 20, 1965, over Telesistema Mexicano and printed as "El control de precios," *El Mercado de Valores* 25 (July 5, 1965), p. 426.

82. Vernon, *Dilemma of Mexico's Development*, p. 126.

83. *Ibid.*

84. A few people maintain that there are still vast amounts of land, illegally held, that should be redistributed.

Chapter II

THE INDUSTRIAL SECTOR

World War II created the necessary conditions which allowed Mexico to accelerate its industrial growth. The industrial nucleus that existed at the beginning of the war included such basic industries as iron and steel, electric power, petroleum, mining, cement, and textiles. From 1925-40, 70 percent of the gross fixed public investment was directed toward improving and expanding the network of railroads and roads.[1] The improvements in the railway system proved to be particularly important, as the additional traffic "during the war years from 1940 to 1944 was achieved mainly by more intensive use of railroad equipment."[2] In 1940, 12.7 percent of the labor force was employed in industry, and 24.7 percent of the GNP was accounted for by mining, petroleum, manufacturing, construction, and electric power. (See Tables 3 and 4.)

"At the beginning of World War II, there was much unused industrial capacity in Mexico."[3] The supply of capital goods available for export to Mexico was curtailed, and the growth in industrial production during the war years was, to a large extent, the result of using existing facilities more intensively. The Combined Mexican Working Party reported that from 1939 to 1946 the volume of industrial production, adjusted to correct for price changes, rose 74.6 percent, with industrial production for the domestic market and industrial exports increasing 62.0 percent and 805.4 percent, respectively.[4]

Table 10 shows the increases in industrial production from 1946 to 1969. Because of revisions that have been made in the industrial production index, it is not possible to construct a consistent unified series on industrial production that covers the entire period from 1940 through 1969. The national income accounts, however, show that industrial output measured in 1950 pesos registered approximately a 6.5-fold advance from 1940 to 1964 and rose an additional 37 percent from 1964 to 1968. The industrial labor force expanded approximately 4.3-fold from 1940 to 1967. The industrial sector grew faster than any other segment of the economy and absorbed labor faster than any other activity except private and government services.[5]

The rate of industrial growth, however, has been declining over this period. The compound annual rate of growth was almost 10 percent from 1940 to 1950, nearly 7 percent from 1950 to 1960, about 5 percent from 1960 to 1964, and somewhat over 5 percent from 1964 to 1969. The decline in the rate of growth in the industrial labor force has been more moderate. The Mexican Government has been concerned with the country's industrial development and has taken numerous measures to promote and direct the industrial sector.

Channels for Communication and Consultation between the Government and Business

While the Mexican Government has been particularly interested in increasing industrial production, the PRI does not have a sector that specifically represents and promotes the interests of the business community. Furthermore, there has been no significant effort to incorporate the leadership of the industrial community within the party structure, as other meaningful lines of communication and consultation have been established.

Concerning the relationship between government and business, one observer of Mexican politics has written:

> In fact, by far the largest proportion of organizations associated with nonagricultural economic activity, be it manufacturing, processing, or commercial, are related to the decision making process not voluntarily but because they are legally required to. According to laws enacted in 1936, 1941, and 1950, every industry or business capitalized at over 500 pesos must belong to one of the fifty-odd functionally specialized chambers grouped together in the National Federation of Industrial Chambers (Confederación de Cámaras Industriales, or CONCAMIN) or 250 geographically based chambers organized nationally as the Federation of National Chambers of Commerce (Confederación de Cámaras Nacionales de Comercio, or CONCANACO), depending upon the nature of the function performed.[6]

Beyond this, the government, through the Secretaría de Industria y Comercio, is empowered to settle any dispute as to what chamber a given firm should join, and it has the authority to determine what functional chambers of CONCAMIN should be established. The Secretaría also sends observers to all national meetings of either chamber. "Failure [on the part of an individual member of either *confederación*] to pay dues constitutes cause for Government prosecution for tax evasion."[7]

These two national *confederaciones* have been dominated by the larger, more solidly established firms. From the formation of these *confederaciones* during the term of President Cárdenas until the late

The Industrial Sector 37

1940s or early 1950s, both groups expressed strong opposition to any government intervention in the economy. A group of small manufacturers within CONCAMIN who had less potential for obtaining credits and were fearful of foreign competition organized a separate organization, the Cámara Nacional de la Industria de Transformación (National Chamber of Manufacturing Industries), which generally supported the government's interventionist and protectionist economic policies.

Following World War II, CONCAMIN's official position shifted, and it began "requesting more protection for industry, more tax exemptions for new lines of production, a system of export subsidies for manufactures, and various other standard forms of government assistance to industry."[8] CONCANACO, for its part, gradually accepted government regulation in certain areas, but concentrated its energy on attacking intervention in the domestic market, particularly the buying and selling of basic foodstuffs.[9] By 1960, CONCANACO had softened its opposition to governmental interference in this area and entered into an agreement with CEIMSA which provided that individual members could distribute certain foodstuffs at the officially fixed prices.

There is also a voluntary organization of employers called the Confederación Patronal de la República Mexicana (Employers' Confederation). In the early 1960s it had a membership of approximately 10,000[10] and provided various services to its members including "seminars on such subjects as productivity, human relations, and industrial relations, and advice on labor-management relations."[11]

The Legal Basis for Promoting Industrial Development

Contacts between government officials and individual businessmen became increasingly desirable and inevitable for both parties as specific legislation was enacted that had a direct bearing on the profitability of existing or potential firms. While 1940 and the years immediately following are generally thought to mark an important shift toward industrialization, various governmental measures to foster industrial production were undertaken in prior years. "As early as 1920, the government announced its intention along this line by passing a law giving tax relief and import duty exemptions to certain new industrial ventures."[12] Presidential decrees reaffirming and broadening the 1920 law were issued in 1926, 1932, and 1939, and these decrees were codified in the 1941 Ley de Industrias de Transformación (Law of Manufacturing Industries).

The 1941 Ley de Industrias de Transformación which permitted certain tax exemptions for a five-year period to enterprises that manufactured either new or necessary products was superseded by the 1946 Ley de

Fomento de Industrias de Transformación (Law for the Development of Manufacturing Industries) "which established three categories of industries to which tax concessions could be granted and also extended the duration of the concession period to ten years."[13] This law also provided for tariff concessions on the importation of machinery and raw materials needed by these firms. Another interesting feature of this law is that:
> tax exemptions granted to a new enterprise or to an established concern which expands, are automatically applicable to all other firms in the same industry even if they have been in existence for many years and are making no new investments. Moreover, there is nothing in the law which would prevent an established firm which is planning no new investment from applying and obtaining tax exemptions.[14]

The *Memoria* of the Secretaría de Economía covering the period from September, 1950, to August, 1951, recorded that 55 firms with capitalization ranging from 8,500 pesos to 35,000,000 pesos qualified for tax exemptions under this law.[15]

In 1955, the Ley de Fomento de Industrias Nuevas y Necesarias (Law for the Development of New and Necessary Industries) came into effect and still constitutes one of the most important legal tools available to the government for promoting and influencing industrial development.[16] This particular piece of legislation is designed to further a number of the government's major policy objectives. It authorized exemption from or reduction of various taxes if firms produce either "articles not already being produced within the country, so long as these goods are not mere substitutes for existing products, and provided that these new industries contribute materially to the economic development of the country"[17] or "goods already being produced in the country, but in quantities insufficient to meet the needs of the nation, provided the deficit is substantial and not due to temporary causes."

There are stipulated procedures for determining a substantial deficit in the apparent need of a given commodity which relates the percentage of imports to total domestic consumption for a given period. The effort to substitute domestically produced goods for foreign goods represents another aspect of making Mexico self-sufficient and is frequently justified as being one means of protecting the country's foreign exchange position.

Obviously, import substitution by itself was considered to be a sufficient justification for government intervention. No procedures were established to determine priorities or to weigh the overall cost advantages of importing a particular commodity as opposed to producing it domestically. The basic principles of foreign trade and, in particular, the law of comparative advantage played no official role in the

The Industrial Sector

decision-making process.

The legislation to promote industrial development, as well as the legal procedures to accelerate agricultural development, gave vast discretionary authority to the executive branch of government. The Secretaría de Industria y Comercio was to determine if a firm qualifies for the protection and incentives provided by this legislation.

From the early years of Mexico's industrialization until the early 1960's, new manufacturing enterprises had been established in Mexico with little regard to the effect on prices. Early in the 1960's an informal guideline was applied in certain cases to restrain undue price rises derived from import substitution; namely, that domestic manufacture should not result in more than a 35% price increase.

The Díaz Ordaz Administration, however, set more rigorous conditions. Its rule, which seems to have been applied consistently since mid-1965, is that a new manufacturing enterprise will not be allowed to produce at prices higher than 15 to 25%—depending on the circumstances of the industry—above the prices prevailing in the country of origin of the corresponding import. A maximum of 10% has even been specified for certain enterprises.[18]

These changes do not indicate that industrialization has become less important as an official objective but stem from Mexico's need to reduce inflationary pressures, to broaden the potential market, both domestic and international, for domestically produced manufactured or semiprocessed goods, and to improve the international competitive position of these products. Many Mexican officials apparently believe that a program to expand exports of manufactured or semiprocessed goods would be the most economically and politically feasible method to acquire the necessary foreign exchange to pay for the rising volume of imported capital goods, to service the country's sizable foreign debt,[19] and to maintain aggregated demand at a sufficiently high level to allow for further industrial development and continued economic growth.[20]

Mexico's keen desire to develop foreign markets has brought about a relaxation in its policy of not entering into international agreements that would limit its power to restrict the flow of international trade. Mexico's decision to join the Latin American Free Trade Area in 1960 marked a major shift in its international trade policy. As it has become increasingly clear that LAFTA was not bringing about the gains that many had expected at the time of its formation, Mexico has undertaken a leading role in diplomatic maneuvers to explore the possibility of expanding trade with the Central American Common Market[21] and forming a Latin American Common Market.[22] On the domestic front, the government has reduced export taxes and has established facilities to aid in the financing of exports.[23]

These initiatives to open foreign markets to Mexican products and to make Mexican goods more competitive reflect the government's realization that the relatively small domestic market where many peasants add little to total aggregate demand creates a definite restriction on the growth of industrial production, particularly of capital goods. There has been an increasing awareness that with the present and foreseeable domestic market, import substitution programs will provide decreasing stimulus to industrial development. Furthermore, there has been, in recent years, an increased awareness of the fact that it is less expensive for Mexico to import certain goods than to produce them domestically, and the government has begun the politically difficult process of reducing tariff barriers to the importation of certain goods. Obviously, measures designed to encourage the substitution of domestically produced goods for any commodity which was "heavily" imported have led to the misallocation of resources.

In regard to this problem, the following passage from a report reviewing the activities of the Secretaría de Industria y Comercio is relevant:

> The appearance of production and distribution problems in some branches of industry, derived principally from excess capacity in relation to the ability of the market to absorb it, has necessitated systematic state intervention to prevent the phenomenon of overproduction and with it the waste of resources.[24]

It should be clearly understood, however, that recent decisions placing greater emphasis on market forces have been administrative and not legislative decisions. Perhaps the desire to accelerate Mexico's economic growth will bring about greater reliance on market forces, but there is, of course, no assurance that future decision makers will stress market forces.

There are two other measures that give the government broad authority for direct intervention in the industrial sector. One device, used on only a few occasions, gives the government power to declare that a given productive activity has become saturated. By declaring a given activity saturated, in either a specific region or throughout the country, the government forbids new firms to enter into that particular field of endeavor. For example, wheat milling was declared saturated throughout Mexico in 1963. Prior to that time, it was considered saturated only in the Federal District.[25]

The other measure is the law entitled *Atribuciones del Ejecutivo Federal en Materia Económica.* The provisions of this law are so vague and sweeping that virtually any firm engaged in an industrial or commercial activity could be subject to far-reaching direct governmental intervention. While this law authorizes the government to eliminate unnecessary middlemen, to establish priorities among the production of industrial commodities, to control the distribution of products, and to assure that no exportation of raw materials occurs before the needs of the domestic market are satisfied, the greatest public attention has probably been focused on measures dealing with price[26] and import controls.

Import Controls

Tariffs and import licensing have played critical roles in Mexico's economic development since the end of World War II. Import controls have been applied in an attempt to shield domestic industry from possible foreign competition, to reduce potential demands against the country's gold and foreign exchange, to raise revenue, and to further a number of other government objectives.

By threats to curtail its import permits, one big American chemical company is now being pressured into manufacturing insecticides in Mexico instead of importing them. Import permits are also used to compel importers of soda ash to get 25 per cent of their supplies from Poland, so that Mexico can comply with its trade agreement with Poland.

In other cases, import permits have been used in combination with other administrative controls such as loans and stock issues, and on the importation of foreign executives or technicians, to produce a higher percentage of Mexican ownership, to control prices not already controlled by law, and to force new plants to be built outside the crowded metropolitan area.[27]

Tariff rates are set by the Secretaría de Hacienda y Crédito Público (Ministry of the Treasury and Public Credit) and are not an insignificant source of revenue.[28] "In fixing individual tariff rates, the Secretaría de Hacienda has no specific norms or uniform criteria. Each application for the alteration of a rate is dealt with individually."[29] Quantitative import controls are administered by the Secretaría de Industria y Comercio. As the dominant goals being pursued by the two ministries at any given time have not always coincided, the use of these basic import control tools has not always been coordinated.

In 1959, the government established an executive committee to maintain effective control over imports by the government and public agencies. There are formal procedures whereby representatives of the private sector advise the government on the establishment of tariff policy. Of course, individual private businessmen have been deeply enmeshed in efforts to raise or lower tariff rates or to broaden or restrict import permits on specific products that either compete with goods they produce or are inputs in their productive process.

The Mexicanization of Industry

Since the overthrow of Porfirio Díaz, the Mexican Government has been suspicious of foreign ownership, fearing a possible loss of independence through foreign domination or "exploitation" of its resources. While a number of measures have been used to promote Mexican control of the Mexican economy, the two most publicized aspects of this program have been (1) a presidential decree, issued in 1944, which gave the government discretionary authority to require 51 percent Mexican ownership in all Mexican companies, and (2) nationalization. There is, however, a decree, which was also issued in 1944, providing that "operations by which Mexican nationals acquired foreign-owned enterprises were exempt from the income tax—a further inducement for Mexicanization."[30]

The literature concerning the government's authority to require 51 percent Mexican ownership suggests that this policy has been carried out with increasing determination over the years.[31] Even when the government used this authority sparingly, the threat that it could be used elsewhere was an incentive for foreigners to acquire Mexican partners. This stimulus has increased as the government has intensified its efforts to Mexicanize the economy.

Not long ago, Manuel Espinosa Yglesias, the chief executive officer of a large commercial bank, "warned against efforts to 'Mexicanize' foreign-controlled companies."[32] He argued that this policy reduced the domestic capital available for establishing new industries and thereby limited potential production and jobs for Mexico's expanding population. This position was opposed by many of Mexico's leading industrialists who maintained that the government was too lax in carrying out the Mexicanization program.[33] The debate concerning this policy was so important that Díaz Ordaz said in his second State of the Union message:

> Lacking sufficient capital to attain adequate rates of economic growth, we have already stated that we conditionally accept foreign investment as a complement to national investment.
>
> To dispense with external resources is the thesis of those who, enjoying high standards of living, do not suffer the consequences of retardation in our development, which would fall hardest on those with the most limited incomes. Those who would like to open the door to foreign investment, without limit or safeguards, forget that with our economic development we try to consolidate, to the greatest extent possible, national independence; we aspire to a development with independence and social well-being.[34]

While this policy appealed to the nationalistic interests of the Mexican people, it curtailed to some degree the volume of foreign investment funds. The mining industry proved an example of how this policy worked against the objective of greater industrialization. Legislation enacted in the early 1960s to reduce the substantial tax burden on the mining industry applied only to companies controlled by Mexican capital.[35] In addition, government administrators were given considerable discretionary power in applying this legislation.

Whether a given company gets a reduction of 50 or 75 per cent depends upon its skill in negotiating with the Government when it receives its mining concessions. Even then, such concessions are of limited duration, and must be renegotiated every few years according to the terms of the concession.[36]

The outcome of this legislation was that the volume of mining production at the end of 1965 was only modestly above the level recorded in 1960. (See Table 10.)

Nationalization

Nationalization has been used mainly where the government believed that Mexican ownership of certain facilities was vital to the country's welfare or where the private sector seemed unable, for a variety of reasons, to operate given enterprises successfully. In 1908 the Mexican Government bought controlling interests from foreign owners in the main railroad lines.[37] In 1937 and 1938, government ownership of the railroad system was extended by presidential decree in an effort to prevent total collapse of this important segment of the economy.[38] The oil industry was nationalized by President Cárdenas in a dramatic confrontation in 1938. In the same year, legislation was passed that established government regulation of the electric power industry, which was at that time controlled mainly by foreign interests. The ensuing relationship between the government and private electric companies was not a harmonious one.[39] Regulation was designed to keep the price of electricity as low as possible, and the government became an active participant in the production of electricity. The electric industry came under complete government control in 1960.

From 1940 to 1970, the government bought control of or established an impressive array of enterprises in widely scattered areas of industrial activity.[40] Government ownership of the telegraph system, aviation facilities, ships and port facilities, and the telephone system reflect the continuing intent to build up the infrastructure of the economy. The purchases of the exhibition contracts of two major movie chains and a large steel mill, La Consolidada, during the term of López Mateos suggest that the government's dominant motive was to buy out foreign ownership.[41] Control of other enterprises may be ascribed to a variety of other motives ranging from promoting import substitution to preventing the failure of a given firm.

By listing all of the economic activities in which the government directly participates, it is possible to state that "Mexico has steadily acquired equity in one sector of economic activity after another."[42]

Table 10

Index of Industrial Production, 1945-69
(1945=100 and 1950=100 and 1960=100)[a]

Year	Total production	Mining	Petroleum	Manufacturing	Construction	Electric energy
1946	100.1	73.8	110.0	102.0	113.2	108.1
1947	103.2	94.2	129.0	103.0	93.2	117.3
1948	106.1	84.5	129.4	107.1	104.9	129.3
1949	111.3	84.9	141.0	111.0	126.7	141.1
1950	122.7	92.4	153.5	121.4	154.2	144.2
1951	130.1	87.8	169.4	128.7	172.6	160.0
1951	109.0	96.4	110.0	110.6	109.5	111.0
1952	115.7	107.0	116.0	115.5	123.3	120.7
1953	114.1	105.9	117.8	114.2	113.8	128.9
1954	123.1	99.8	126.8	125.3	122.5	142.0
1955	135.8	115.6	136.8	137.5	136.5	158.3
1956	150.0	116.8	146.0	153.1	157.6	177.0
1957	161.0	124.5	155.5	163.1	178.3	191.1
1958	168.3	123.8	173.8	171.9	172.2	205.7

Table 10 – Continued

Year	Total production	Mining	Petroleum	Manufac- turing	Construc- tion	Electric energy
1959	182.0	127.7	197.0	187.3	176.0	221.0
1960	197.4	132.6	207.8	202.9	201.6	242.6
1961	204.7	127.0	231.4	210.1	203.6	265.6
1961	104.9	95.9	110.9	105.5	99.5	108.9
1962	110.0	102.6	114.3	110.3	106.0	117.4
1963	120.6	105.1	121.2	120.8	121.4	136.3
1964	138.9	107.8	134.2	140.2	141.9	159.4
1965	148.5	107.7	142.8	152.3	139.8	176.1
1966	162.4	111.4	148.9	166.5	159.9	195.8
1967	175.1	114.6	169.1	177.0	180.7	217.7
1968	191.3	121.6	183.8	194.3	194.0	241.8
1969p	207.6	128.7	194.7	211.1	212.0	275.1

aThe top portion of this table is based on 1945=100; the middle portion uses 1950=100; and the lower portion uses 1960=100. While 1951 and 1961 are shown by each method of calculation, the revisions and expanded coverage that necessitates a break in the table have created two separate series. They are pieced together here only to indicate trends.

pPreliminary.

Source: Banco de México, *Informe anual, 1960, 1965,* and *1969,* pp. 75, 91, and 66, respectively.

Implications that the government has been attempting to gain control of the country's means of production,[43] however, are not supported by existing statistics. In 1960, the private sector accounted for 85 percent of the total value of goods and services produced by the industrial sector.[44] Of the remaining 15 percent, electric power and petroleum production represented the major proportion, accounting for 11 percent of the total value of industrial production.

Table 11 shows that public gross fixed investments for industrial development have largely been concentrated in the fields of electric power, petroleum and gas, and communication and transportation. As one source has written: "Irrigation, power, petroleum and transportation were clearly the sectors of highest priority for Mexican public investment, as they had been for twenty years."[45] When President Díaz Ordaz announced the government's investment plans for the period from 1966 to 1970, he indicated that 56 percent of gross public investments would be devoted to electric power, petroleum, and transportation.[46] In 1963, gross public investments directed to these areas accounted for 52 percent of gross fixed public investments.[47]

In allocating investment funds, the government has been devoting greater attention to social investments. (See Table 11.) Investments in this area include low-cost housing for Mexico's ever-expanding population, hospitals and hospital equipment, and educational facilities. Considering the limited resources available to the government and its present commitments, there seems little likelihood that the government would make many drastic changes in regard to the nationalization of industry.

By increasing the supply of electricity, oil, and gas and spreading their availability throughout the country and by improving and expanding the network of railroads, roads, ports, and aviation facilities, the government has attempted to create a foundation upon which an industrialized economy could be built. Many of the large firms having state participation, such as iron and steel mills, cement plants, and a railroad-car manufacturing plant, are necessary for the construction or operation of this foundation. Ownership in other firms such as producers of chemical fertilizers reflect efforts to increase food production, a critical problem with economic and social implications for the country. To a large extent, the government has encouraged the private sector to build upon the foundation that it has created, but the government has, and exercises, power to influence the actions of the private sector.

Financing the Industrial Sector

The government through monetary policy is able to force the private banking system to channel available funds into particular sectors of the

Table 11

Gross Public Fixed Investment for Industrial Development, 1940–70
(Millions of pesos)

Year	Total	Electricity	Petroleum and gas	Iron and steel industry	Mining	Communication and transportation	Social investments (mainly building construction)	Other[a]
1940	246	3	57			152	29	5
1941	278	4	24			189	54	7
1942	400	10	28			300	54	7
1943	482	10	26			387	51	8
1944	535	20	41			388	71	15
1945	704	16	113			460	91	24
1946	806	38	111			526	106	25
1947	1,052	76	85			674	181	36
1948	1,220	99	168			681	241	31
1949	1,498	173	247			785	236	84
1950	2,157	362	398			1,079	256	62

Table 11 - Continued

Year	Total	Electricity	Petroleum and gas	Iron and steel industry	Mining	Communication and transportation	Social investments (mainly building construction)	Other[a]
1951	2,257	263	425			1,158	345	66
1952	2,719	185	369			1,378	600	187
1953	2,513	253	456			1,344	257	203
1954	3,557	331	901	33	2	1,488	391	411
1955	3,803	369	1,055	53	7	1,422	597	300
1956	3,922	285	860	102	17	1,703	856	99
1957	4,958	294	1,283	132		2,018	1,058	173
1958	5,492	462	1,327	154	79	2,377	876	217
1959	5,781	762	957	141	5	2,747	863	306
1960	7,796	1,455	1,046	35	12	3,014	1,885	349
1961	9,421	2,518	1,805	96	20	2,801	1,757	424
1962	10,005	2,291	1,594	130	4	3,119	2,272	595
1963	12,407	1,760	2,001	248	178	3,397	3,982	841
1964	15,266	1,852	2,729	251	40	3,668	5,553	1,172

Table 11 – Continued

Year	Total	Electricity	Petroleum and petrochemical industry	Iron and steel industry	Communication and transportation	Social investments	Other[b]
1965	14,753	1,565	4,107	506	4,320	2,851	1,404
1966	18,742	2,745	5,317	317	5,169	4,569	625
1967	19,673	2,795	5,059	182	5,501	5,033	1,103
1968	21,560	2,950	5,200	335	5,757	6,035	1,283
1969	23,895	3,272	6,569	900	5,782	6,679	693
1970	26,250	4,147	5,440	740	6,500	8,000	1,424

[a]Includes expenditures for other industries with state participation, public buildings, military equipment and facilities, and warehouses.

[b]Includes all of above except warehouses, which are put in agricultural investments for years 1965-70.

Sources: Secretaría de la Presidencia, Dirección de Inversiones Públicas, *México: Inversión pública federal, 1925-1963*, pp. 43-46 and 119, and *México: Inversión pública federal, 1965-1970*, pp. 136-37 and 209.

economy.⁴⁸ In addition, the government has established several national credit institutions, mainly for financing industrial development. Table 12 shows that the industrial sector's share of total credits extended by the Mexican banking system rose sharply from 1942 to 1952 and has constituted approximately somewhat less than 50 percent since that time.

Mexico's financial institutions have developed either because there was a demand for their services or because the government believed that an institution was needed to promote a facet or facets of economic growth. With the growth of various private industrial firms, the needs for investment capital exceeded the supply of internally generated funds. The banking reforms of 1932 authorized the creation of private *financieras* (industrial finance companies) "to provide longer-term finance (usually up to five years)."⁴⁹ Commercial banks were restricted to short-term finance. As demands for industrial credits expanded in the early 1940s, commercial banks were allowed to make longer-term loans and *financieras* were permitted:

> to issue securities for sale to the public, to guarantee security issues of others, to promote the organization and reorganization of business enterprises, to become open or silent partners in firms, to hold all kinds of stocks, bonds, and other credit instruments, to accept time deposits, to grant loans of almost all kinds, to underwrite and trade in securities, and 'in general, to carry out those operations necessary for fulfilling the duties of financing production and placing capital.'⁵⁰

Financieras were still prohibited from engaging in certain functions, such as accepting demand deposits, that are traditionally reserved for commercial banks.

There has been a definite tendency for commercial banks and *financieras* to work in close unison. Concerning this phenomenon, Shelton has written:

> Institutions found it advantageous to band together because they could thereby reduce competitive pressures, enhance profit opportunities, and cushion the impact of Banco de México regulation. Financial 'groups' consisting usually of a major commercial bank, a strong financiera, and lesser insurance, banking, or similar firms have come to dominate private finance. These groups are often allied with a circle of commercial or industrial firms which absorbs a considerable part of the credit which the financial entities are able to provide.⁵¹

While the government has set up a number of national development banks that have a direct impact on the industrial sector,⁵² the Nacional Financiera (National Development Bank) is by far the most important. "Originally established to supervise and regulate the securities market, to act as a savings bank and investment company, and, since 1941

Table 12

Financing by the Mexican Banking System
for Industrial Production,[a] 1942-69

	Total financing (millions of pesos)	Financing for industrial production (millions of pesos)	Industrial financing as a percentage of total financing
1940	n.a.	n.a.	n.a.
1941	n.a.	n.a.	n.a.
1942	2,024.2	491.3	24.3
1943	2,529.6	730.4	28.9
1944	3,249.9	1,053.7	32.4
1945	4,075.7	1,375.2	33.7
1946	4,908.4	1,818.5	37.0
1947	5,748.9	2,361.5	41.1
1948	7,040.8	3,021.6	43.1
1949	8,172.0	3,471.0	42.5
1950	8,972.7	4,035.4	45.0
1951	10,767.3	5,413.3	50.3
1952	11,887.5	5,856.8	49.3
1953	13,497.8	6,665.6	49.4
1954	16,811.4	8,588.9	51.1
1955	17,672.7	8,310.0	47.0
1956	19,675.6	9,203.7	46.8
1957	22,464.0	10,543.7	46.9
1958	26,583.3	12,673.9	47.7
1959	31,369.0	15,144.5	48.4
1960	39,780.5	19,861.7	49.9
1961	46,055.9	24,502.6	53.2
1962	53,454.4	30,776.6	57.6
1963	61,251.5	33,013.7	53.9
1964	74,434.9	38,942.7	52.3

Table 12 - Continued

	Total financing (millions of pesos)	Financing for industrial production (millions of pesos)	Industrial financing as a percentage of total financing
1965	87,374.0	42,275.6	48.4
1966	104,629.5	47,136.7	45.1
1967	121,105.3	56,311.9	46.5
1968	138,767.6	63,654.6	45.9
1969	167,224.9	76,766.7	45.9

[a] Includes credits for mining.

Source: Banco de México, *Informe anual 1969*, p. 102.

particularly, to advise the government in financial transactions, it has played a central role in implementing the government's policy of rapid industrialization."⁵³

In theory, the Nacional Financiera is a mixed enterprise, as the private sector is permitted to own up to 49 percent of its stock. In practice, however, it is controlled by the government. The heads of the Secretaría de Hacienda y Crédito Público, the Secretaría de Industria y Comercio, the Secretaría del Patrimonio Nacional (Ministry of National Properties) and the Banco de México are on the Board of Directors and exercise effective voting control.

The Nacional Financiera has been able to make either direct loans to a firm or provide funds by purchasing stock of a given enterprise. In 1945, Nacional Financiera was "a stockholder in 35 corporations and majority owner of five."⁵⁴ Over the years, it has expanded its activities. "As of mid-1961, it was creditor, investor, or guarantor for 533 business enterprises of all kinds; it held stocks in 60 industrial firms; it was majority stockholder in 13 firms producing steel, textiles, motion pictures, plywood, paper, fertilizers, electrical energy, sugar, lumber, and refrigerated meats."⁵⁵

Because of its size, resources,⁵⁶ and connection with the government, Nacional Financiera has been able to invest substantial sums and resources, such as managerial talent, into the various firms with which it is associated. (Table 13 shows total financing channeled through the Nacional Financiera.) From 1934 to mid-1961, it has "earned some net income in every year."⁵⁷ In fact, its profit record has been used by some to indicate that it has not promoted economic growth as rapidly as it should have.

While the Nacional Financiera does assist private enterprise by making loans to private firms, it has shown no willingness to sell the larger and more successful firms in which it has majority control. It has also been criticized for giving insufficient support to small businesses. Sanford A. Mosk, for example, argued that Mexico was too concerned with "big" enterprises and neglected "smaller" ones.⁵⁸ In 1954, the Fondo de Garantía y Fomento a la Industria Mediana y Pequeña (Fund for the Guarantee and Development of Medium and Small Industry) began operations as a trust fund of the Nacional Financiera. Table 14 gives some idea of the extent of its activities since its creation. Obviously, the credits for medium and small industries are only a small percentage of the total credits extended by Nacional Financiera. (See Table 13.)

Concentration of Industry

As was mentioned in the preceding section, industrial and commercial

Table 13

Total Financing Channeled through the Nacional Financiera, 1940-67[a]
(Thousands of pesos)

End of Year	Total	Infrastructure[b]	Basic industries[c]	Other industries[d]	Other[e]
1940	20,136	3,233	1,337	637	14,929
1941	47,845	26,075	2,294	3,647	15,829
1942	242,953	194,510	16,434	6,215	25,794
1943	472,701	364,413	68,903	16,825	22,650
1944	539,409	338,148	113,089	39,612	48,560
1945	802,385	387,760	213,544	88,256	112,825
1946	936,753	422,764	191,687	140,737	181,565
1947	1,135,090	520,549	197,424	265,376	151,741
1948	1,460,567	655,758	216,767	326,067	261,975
1949	1,789,005	883,027	220,530	364,838	320,610
1950	2,236,940		264,119	382,359	444,441
1951	3,003,516	1,495,709	243,429	465,479	798,899
1952	3,733,500	1,767,500	434,100	537,800	944,100
1953	4,742,400	2,239,900	585,900	707,000	1,209,600
1954	6,063,100	3,084,400	1,043,800	906,300	974,600

Table 13 - Continued

End of Year	Total	Infrastructure[b]	Basic industries[c]	Other industries[d]	Other[e]
1955	6,321,700	3,144,900	1,109,900	1,342,200	724,700
1956	7,077,500	3,422,700	1,033,100	1,740,300	881,400
1957	7,337,700	3,826,300	1,135,500	1,770,000	1,105,900
1958	8,948,700	4,348,800	1,251,500	2,315,200	1,033,200
1959	9,579,800	4,562,400	1,726,000	2,279,200	1,012,200
1960	13,567,500	7,757,800	2,139,600	2,459,100	1,211,000
1961	17,962,000	9,188,500	2,323,700	2,896,800	3,533,000
1962	22,127,000	10,789,600	2,638,600	3,234,100	5,464,700
1963	20,722,700	12,785,800	2,065,100	3,273,800	2,598,000
1964	25,165,500	16,339,300	1,845,900	4,600,500	2,379,800
1965	25,522,900	17,040,600	1,894,500	4,345,200	2,242,600
1966	27,786,200	18,893,200	2,237,500	5,174,400	1,481,100
1967	31,993,300	21,498,900	3,313,100	5,131,700	2,049,600

[a]Total financing includes the sum of credits, investments, guarantees, and credits of trust funds.

[b]Infrastructure includes transportation and communication, electric energy, roads and bridges, irrigation, and other works.

Table 13 - Continued

c Basic industries include petroleum and coal, iron and steel, cement and other construction materials, and nonferrous metals.

d Other industries include food and beverages, textiles and apparel, paper and paper products, fertilizers and chemical products, metal products and machinery, transportation equipment, and others.

e Other includes finance, trade, service industries, government, and any other economic activity not classified elsewhere. The figures for 1961-63 also reflect financing by the Fund for Importing Capital Goods.

Source: "Algunas cifras de Nacional Financiera, S.A." *El Mercado de Valores* (September 19, 1966), pp. 936-37, and Nacional Financiera, *Informe anual 1967*, p. 15.

Table 14

Activities of El Fondo de Garantía y Fomento
a la Industria Mediana y Pequeña, 1954-69

Year	Number of credits authorized	Value of credits in thousands of pesos
1954	99	18,534
1955	349	49,067
1956	375	68,061
1957	432	72,953
1958	488	89,787
1959	613	103,690
1960	589	110,017
1961	703	136,832
1962	699	133,022
1963	670	176,394
1964	672	167,463
1965	749	187,327
1966	790	176,254
1967	757	184,883
1968	786	218,933
1969	864	235,819

Source: "Actividades del Fondo de Garantía y Fomento a la Industria Mediana y Pequeña," *El Mercado de Valores* (May 11, 1970), p. 258.

circles are often closely associated with large financial groups. Frank Brandenburg has listed the major industrial, commercial and financial complexes as including:

Raúl Bailleres (finance, mining, breweries, bottling, and real estate), Carlos Trouyet (finance, telephone, manganese, steels, cellulose and paper, banking, cement, and a host of other activities), the Garza Sada and G. Sada families (the vast Monterrey industrial and commercial complex of beer, glass, chemicals, banking, insurance, finance), Luis Aguilar (banking, pharmaceuticals, real estate, construction materials, consumer goods, wholesale distribution, manufacturing), Emilio Azcárraga (radio, television, hotels, sports arenas), the García family (sugar and finance), Joel Rocha (chain merchandising, supermarkets, chemicals), Antonio Ruiz Galindo (office equipment, truck bodies, coffee, hotels, aluminum), and Bruno Pagliai (steel pipes, finance, real estate, aluminum).[59]

There is a lack of statistical information that would show the overall size of any one of these complexes or would allow meaningful judgments as to whether or not they have in recent years become larger or smaller in relation to the total market.[60]

Summary

Mexico's industrial sector has recorded substantial growth from 1940 through 1970. This growth has been coupled with a remarkable degree of diversification. The diversification has been encouraged by government policies of import substitution and increasing industrialization. In the process, the government has concentrated its resources on efforts to increase the infrastructure of the economy. In particular this has meant sizable investments in electricity, petroleum and gas, and communications and transportation.

The government has not, however, permitted market force to determine allocation of private resources in the industrial area. Only in recent years has there been any real concern regarding the cost to the economy of producing goods domestically rather than importing them. In the past, the government was willing to use tariffs and import licensing to remove foreign competition; it has continued to stress its program of Mexicanization of industry, even though the rate of industrial growth has been slowing down in recent years; and it has given tax reductions and import privileges to industries that it wanted to stimulate. At the same time, government administrators who implemented these policies are permitted to discriminate widely among firms in any particular industry.

Outside of the general area of infrastructure and the basic industries supporting the economy's infrastructure, the government has acquired ownership of individual firms. There has not, however, been any attempt

The Industrial Sector

to own all of the country's means of production.

In the future, industrial growth will continue to be hampered by the limited size of Mexico's effective domestic market. In addition, the rapidly expanding population may force the government to shift investment funds from the industrial sector to social investments. The extent to which Mexico will be able to develop foreign markets for their manufactured or semiprocessed goods remains to be seen, but, at the present time, it must be assumed that successes in this area will be modest and slow in fruition.

Notes

1. Computed from: Secretaría de la Presidencia, Dirección de Inversiones Públicas, *México: Inversión pública federal, 1925-63*, pp. 41-43.

2. Combined Mexican Working Party, *Economic Development of Mexico*, p. 88.

3. *Ibid.*, p. 63.

4. *Ibid.*, computed from Table 78, p. 276.

5. It is generally believed that there is substantial underemployment in the services area. It seems obvious that the government deliberately "overemploys" in a number of areas. The sales force for the National Lottery is a case in point.

6. Robert E. Scott, *Mexican Government in Transition*, p. 284.

7. Arthur Neef, *Labor Law and Practice in Mexico*, p. 37.

8. Raymond Vernon, *The Dilemma of Mexico's Development*, p. 167.

9. See Chapter I, pp. 21-26, for a discussion of government intervention in pricing and marketing foodstuffs.

10. Neef, p. 37.

11. *Ibid.*

12. William P. Glade and Charles W. Anderson, *The Political Economy of Mexico*, p. 85.

13. Combined Mexican Working Party, p. 80.

14. *Ibid.*, p. 81.

The Industrial Sector

15. See pp. 96-97.

16. Secretaría de Industria y Comercio, *Memoria de labores, 1959-64*, p. 15.

17. This quotation and the following one are from Rafael Martínez de Escobar, *How to Do Business in Mexico*, pp. 156-57.

18. Douglas K. Ballentine, "The Door Opens Wider: New Administration Reviews Nation's Import Policies; Some Restrictions Eased," *International Commerce* (U.S. Department of Commerce, June 6, 1966), p. 16. President Echeverría Alvarez has already indicated he will continue with the general thrust of this import policy.

19. President Díaz Ordaz said in his second State of the Union message that the total foreign debt of Mexico's public sector amounted to $1,771.1 million as of Dec. 31, 1965. See *Comercio Exterior* 16 (Sept., 1966), p. 653.

20. Ballentine, pp. 15-16.

21. "Mexican President Offers Aid to Honduras," *Financial Times*, February 2, 1966, p. 7, and Henry W. Goethals, "Mexican Expansion Studied," *Christian Science Monitor*, February 19, 1966, p. 16.

22. "Mexicans Pin Hopes on Latin Trade," *Journal of Commerce*, May 23, 1963, p. 11.

23. "Ayudas para la exportación de productos manufacturados," *El Mercado de Valores* (July 18, 1966), pp. 697-704.

24. *Memoria de labores, 1959-64*, p. 20.

25. *Ibid.*, p. 23.

26. See Chapter I, pp. 25-26.

27. "Mexican Import Controls," *Economist*, August 8, 1964, p. 578.

28. See Chapter IV, p. 98.

29. Rafael Izquierdo, "Protectionism in Mexico," *Public Policy and Private Enterprise in Mexico*, edited by Raymond Vernon, p. 254.

30. Glade and Anderson, p. 89.

31. See Edward R. Barlow, *Management of Foreign Manufacturing Subsidiaries*; Daniel Seligman, "The Maddening Promising Mexican Market," *Fortune* 53 (January, 1956); Edmund K. Faltermayer, "We're Bullish on Mexico," *Fortune* 72 (September, 1965); James C. Tanner, "Curbing Yanqui Cash," *Wall Street Journal*, June 17, 1965; Richard L. Barovick, "Joint Ventures in Mexico on the Rise," *Journal of Commerce*, July 19, 1966.

32. Henry Giniger, "Mexican Scores Take-over Moves," *New York Times*, June 27, 1966, p. 51.

33. Paul A. Ollervides, "Sobre la nacionalización y la inversión de capitales extranjeros en la industria," *El Correo Económico*, July 25, 1966, pp. 8-10.

34. *Comercio Exterior* 16 (September, 1966), p. 652.

35. See Katherine E. Rice, "Mexico Enacts Subsidies, Tax Cuts to Stimulate Lagging Mine Industry," *International Commerce* (August 26, 1963), p. 28.

36. "Mexican Mining Tax Refunds Simplified," *Financial Times*, January 13, 1966, p. 7.

37. Vernon, *Dilemma of Mexico's Development*, p. 40.

38. Glade and Anderson, p. 76.

39. Miguel S. Wionczek, "Electric Power: The Uneasy Partnership," *Public Policy and Private Enterprise*, ed. Vernon, pp. 19-110.

40. Secretaría de Industria y Comercio, Dirección General de Estadística, *VII censo industrial: 1960, resumen general*, pp. xxxv-xxxvi, lists forty-one firms having state participation and decentralized agencies engaged in mining or manufacturing, except for petroleum.

41. Vernon, *Dilemma of Mexico's Development*, p. 120.

42. Frank R. Brandenburg, *The Development of Latin American Private Enterprise*, p. 60.

43. Brandenburg, "A Contribution to the Theory of Entrepreneurship and Economic Development: The Case of Mexico," *Inter-American Economic Affairs* 16 (Winter, 1962), p. 9.

44. Secretaría de Industria y Comercio, *VII censo industrial*, p. xxxvii.

45. Albert Waterston, *Development Planning: Lessons of Experience*, p. 73.

46. Calculated from figures given in his second State of the Union message, *Comercio Exterior* 16 (September, 1966), p. 649.

47. Calculated from Tables 11 and 25.

48. Chapter III discusses Mexico's financial system.

49. David F. V. Ashby, "Mexico — Model for Latin America?" *The Banker* 115 (August, 1965), p. 537.

50. David H. Shelton, "The Banking System: Money and the Goal of Growth," *Public Policy and Private Enterprise*, edited by Raymond Vernon, p. 152. Shelton's quotation is cited as *Legislación bancaria*, IV, p. 42.

51. *Ibid.*, p. 120.

52. These would include Banco Nacional de Comercio Exterior, Banco Hipotecario Urbano y de Obras Públicas (Public Works Bank), Banco Nacional de Fomento Cooperativo (Bank of Cooperative Development), and Banco Nacional de Transportes.

53. Glade and Anderson, p. 187.

54. Calvin P. Blair, "Nacional Financiera: Entrepreneurship in a Mixed Economy," *Public Policy and Private Enterprise*, edited by Raymond Vernon, p. 213.

55. *Ibid.*, p. 194.

56. Nacional Financiera's paid-in capital rose from 7.9 million pesos in 1940 to 682.4 million pesos in 1962. See *Anuario financiero de México, 1962*, p. 201.

57. Blair, p. 204.

58. See his work *Industrial Revolution in Mexico*, especially pp. 304-7.

59. *Making of Modern Mexico*, p. 220.

60. Brandenburg, *Development of Latin American Private Enterprise*, p. 62.

Chapter III

THE FINANCIAL SYSTEM

Some degree of governmental regulation of money and financial institutions has become generally accepted throughout the world. Furthermore, it is not uncommon for a government to make special provisions to try to provide credits, perhaps at a "low" rate of interest, for certain purposes.[1] In Mexico, the government is deeply involved in regulating the availability of credit, influencing the level of interest rates, providing direct financing for a wide variety of agricultural, industrial, and commercial activities, influencing the distribution of private banking funds to various sectors of the economy, maintaining the solvency of the banking system and the individual banks, and improving the financial markets.

Structure of the Financial System

Mexico's financial system collapsed during the turmoil that followed the downfall of Porfirio Díaz. The government was faced with the task of rebuilding public confidence in financial institutions, assuring that there were adequate credit facilities to meet the needs of the country, and reaching an understanding with bankers. The process of reconstituting the monetary system was begun by President Álvaro Obregón. As a result of the leadership of President Elías Calles, new banking legislation appeared in 1924 and 1925. The central bank, the Banco de México, was established in 1925, and the Banco Nacional de Crédito Agrícola was created in 1926.

For a long time, the commercial bank had been the dominant institution in the private financial system. *Financieras,* which were authorized to provide longer-term credit to industry, grew rapidly following World War II and have become the largest financial institution in terms of total resources.[2] Mortgage banks, which finance and guarantee mortgage certificates in connection with residential and public construction, are the third most important private financial banking institution. While there are a number of other private banks, collectively they hold a very small percentage of the total resources of the private banking system.

To cope with certain problems confronting the economy, the government has also created a number of national credit institutions to provide financing for some particular areas of the economy.[3] Frequently, national credit institutions will have special trusts that are set up for quite specific purposes.[4] In some cases, national credit institutions are established because the private sector is unwilling or unable, because of the risks involved, to satisfy a particular demand. In other cases the government creates national credit institutions to supply credit to particular economic activities, even though the demand for this credit is not significant.

> 'Supply-leading' has two functions: to transfer resources from traditional (non-growth) sectors to modern sectors, and to promote and stimulate an entrepreneurial response in these modern sectors. Financial intermediation which transfers resources from traditional sectors, whether by collecting wealth and savings from those sectors in exchange for its deposits and other financial liabilities, or by credit creation and forced savings, is akin to the Schumpeterian concept of innovation financing.[5]

The efforts of some of Mexico's national banks, particularly the Nacional Financiera, have certainly fulfilled the "supply-leading" functions.

The national credit institutions have been organized in a conscious attempt to assure that their goals are within the framework of the President's program. In addition, the Secretaría de Hacienda y Crédito Público, one of the most powerful ministries in the President's cabinet, has been delegated primary responsibility for the regulation and development of the Mexican financial system. While the Banco de México has the traditional powers and responsibilities of a central bank, it is not independent within government but an instrument of the government. The actions of the Banco de México are subject to the approval of the Secretaría de Hacienda y Crédito Público, "but since Bank of Mexico-Treasury cooperation has always been very close, this veto has never been exercised."[6] The Comisión Nacional Bancaria and the Comisión Nacional de Valores (National Securities Commission) also function under the general direction of the Secretaría de Hacienda y Crédito Público.

> The Comisión Nacional de Valores regulates the issuance of new private securities, authorizes registry in the security exchanges, and may set coupon rates of interest. It also regulates the operation of private investment trusts (mutual funds). Since the Banco de México and the principal development bank, Nacional Financiera, continually intervene in the securities markets, the Comisión Nacional de Valores must work closely with these institutions. Its decisions often reflect their general policies and aims.

The Financial System

The Comisión Nacional Bancaria is the supervisory agency for technical aspects of bank operation. Mexico's banking laws provide for detailed regulation of many asset and liability categories, and the Comisión Nacional Bancaria must interpret, apply, and enforce these laws. It is also in a position to determine compliance with the Banco de México's edicts, and cooperates closely in implementing the Bank's intricate selective credit controls.[7]

The labyrinth of controls on the private financial system is generally justified on two grounds: to foster economic growth and to enhance public confidence in the financial system. The development of viable and resilient money and capital markets requires financial institutions that enjoy the confidence of the public. One means of cultivating confidence in financial institutions has been the government's unwritten but clearly understood policy that there will be no bank failures. Today "nobody thinks of a bank failure in Mexico; such a contingency is virtually impossible."[8] Assurance that a depositer or a shareholder will not suffer losses because of a bank failure is one means of encouraging deposits and stock ownership, but this assurance apparently brings with it careful government surveillance of banking institutions. The government has not, however, attempted to maintain control of any private bank that has required assistance.[9]

Financial institutions, as was pointed out in Chapter II, tend to form close associations with each other and particular industrial or commercial enterprises. To prevent financial institutions from serving only "affiliated" firms, the government regulates the amount of credit that can be extended to a single enterprise. To encourage savings, "a high degree of liquidity [at or near par] for nonmonetary indirect securities and for fixed-interest primary securities [has been maintained] during the past two decades."[10] Underlying many of the controls and regulations is the desire on the part of the government first to establish confidence in the country's financial institutions and then to promote the development of an increasingly sophisticated money and capital market in which a wide spectrum of the population will have a vested interest.

The vast majority of Mexico's financial institutions are owned by Mexicans. In early 1966, the government passed new legislation "eliminating any chance of foreign takeovers of Mexican financial institutions."[11] This law did not, however, affect the one United States commercial bank that has branches in Mexico nor did it change the status of representative offices maintained in Mexico by foreign commercial banks.

Official Channel for Communication with the Government

Virtually all of Mexico's banks and bankers are associated with the

Asociación de Banqueros de México. This group has traditionally provided a forum where bankers could express their viewpoint in regard to various government policies. The banking industry, on the whole, remained rather hostile to the government's basic economic programs until about a decade ago. Vernon stated: "Even the staid and sober Asociación de Banqueros was bending with the times by the year 1962. Its propaganda in that year emphasized the need of its members to cooperate with the government in solving Mexico's economic problems."[12]

Government regulation of the financial system obviously necessitated contacts between the government and financial leaders. Private bankers originally sought to limit the power and scope of the Banco de México and considered competition from national credit institutions to be unfair, but over the years they have developed mutually beneficial relationships with the Banco de México and many of the national credit institutions. The Banco de México "in a sense represents the private banks before political leadership."[13] In line with the efforts to incorporate, at least on a legal basis, the most important segments of Mexican society into the decision-making process, the government made provisions for the Asociación de Banqueros de México to appoint "some of the members of the National Banking Commission, the National Securities Commission and the Stock Exchange."[14] The government, however, exercises effective control over these agencies.

The Financial System and Economic Growth

While long-term goals are "directed towards a sound structure of financial institutions and of the domestic debt," there is the ever-present concern to "promote rapid and steady economic growth."[15] As was mentioned earlier, the government has established a number of development banks to stimulate economic growth in various sectors of the economy. The Banco de México, through its power to issue currency, has, of course, been able to influence changes in the money supply. The compound annual rate of growth in the money supply, defined as currency outstanding and demand deposits, from 1940 to 1969 was 41.2 percent. (See Table 15.) The money supply expanded most rapidly (24.6 percent annual rate) during Ávila Camacho's administration. The annual rate of growth was approximately 11 percent during the Miguel Alemán and Ruiz Cortines sexennials, about 12 percent during the term of López Mateos, and approximately 12.0 during Díaz Ordaz's years in office. The growing importance of the checking account component of the money supply provides some evidence of increasing public confidence in financial institutions.

The highly liquid nature of domestic indebtedness has resulted in a

Table 15

Money Supply and Fixed-Interest Securities
Outstanding, 1940-69

(Millions of pesos)

	Money supply[a]	Checking accounts	Fixed-interest securities outstanding[b]
1940	943	329	n.a.
1941	1,219	520	n.a.
1942	1,510	633	n.a.
1943	2,283	1,069	n.a.
1944	3,023	1,424	n.a.
1945	3,581	1,828	1,922.8
1946	3,529	1,889	2,409.1
1947	3,416	1,779	2,812.1
1948	3,632	1,814	3,177.1
1949	4,054	1,946	3,542.9
1950	5,405	2,491	4,701.3
1951	6,402	3,390	5,501.8
1952	6,553	3,234	6,338.2
1953	7,167	3,672	7,145.0
1954	7,790	3,808	7,915.8
1955	9,442	4,879	9,275.6
1956	10,602	5,563	10,239.1
1957	11,529	6,149	11,969.8
1958	13,389	6,774	14,192.7
1959	15,434	8,184	15,091.9
1960	16,889	9,014	18,277.3
1961	18,007	9,732	20,376.1
1962	20,274	11,130	22,839.4
1963	23,680	13,416	27,256.9
1964	27,640	15,716	37,327.3
1965	29,519	17,012	53,014.0
1966	32,751	19,122	68,590.7

Table 15 - Continued

	Money supply[a]	Checking accounts	Fixed-interest securities outstanding[b]
1967	35,387	20,638	83,173.0
1968	39,991	23,317	97,603.0
1969	44,635	26,095	111,214.2

[a] Yearly average for 1940-1957 and end of year from 1958-1969.

[b] As of December 31 of each year.

Sources: Nacional Financiera, *50 años de revolución mexicana en cifras*, p. 117; Comisión Nacional de Valores, *Memoria anual, 1964*, p. 90; Banco de México, *Informe anual, 1963* and *1969*, pp. 115 and 117, and p. 103, respectively.

The Financial System

substantial increase in "near money." From 1945 to 1969, advances in fixed-interest securities oustanding exceeded the growth in the money supply. The government has developed techniques to limit the obviously inflationary impact of a rapidly growing money supply and a domestic debt market where "the whole structure resembles a 'call money' market almost without regard to the technical maturities of the various instruments employed."[16] An indication of the unwillingness of most Mexican investors to assume the risks associated with a variable-income security is expressed in the following quotation:

> It is true that there are a dozen industrial firms whose stock enjoy recognized prestige, but these obviously are not enough to make a real securities market. Of the total securities traded in the Mexico City Stock Exchange, industrial shares accounted for only 2 per cent in 1958, 2.9 per cent in 1960, and 1.8 per cent in the first half of 1961.[17]

Many enterprises and groups of enterprises are controlled by closeknit family groups who are reluctant to sell stock to outside interests. This factor also limits the development of a market in common stocks. The Mexicanization of industry has been defended as a means of developing a market in common stocks. It has been felt that Mexicans would be more willing to invest in companies that have substantial foreign backing in terms of money and know-how. For example, in early 1966, "the Mexican affiliate of Anderson, Clayton—the food and fiber processor—went public through the Mexican stock exchange with a $6.4 million [U.S. dollars] issue to raise funds for its expanding operations. It was the biggest public stock issue in Mexico's history."[18] In another instance, a Mexican firm "underwrote an issue of 600,000 common shares last April for Cannon Mills, S.A., at 10.5 pesos (84c) a share."[19]

Changes in reserve requirements, either on the basis of total deposits or deposits acquired after a given date, have been the most effective instrument of monetary policy. According to Bennett:

> The power of the Banco de México to require 100 per cent reserves for increments in deposit liabilities (both demand and time deposits of all private intermediatires) and to specify the financial claims which qualify as reserves makes it possible for Banco de México to prevent multiple expansion for the money supply resulting from the open market operations necessary for maintaining the liquidity of bonds.[20]

"The classical example of application of reserve requirements, so as to regulate not only the quantity, but also the disttribution, of bank credit, has been offered by the Banco de México."[21] In effect, private financial institutions are given the option of either maintaining marginal reserve requirements of 100 percent or agreeing to distribute credits among potential borrowers along government-determined lines. Thus, the government is not only able to force funds into "production" credits rather than trade credits but is also able to regulate the flow of funds from private financial institutions to particular sectors of the economy. For example, by modifying marginal reserve requirements, the Banco de México could bring about a shift in private bank assets that would result in increased (decreased) holdings of government securities and more (less) credits to the agricultural sector as opposed to trade credits. Furthermore, the Banco de México could change marginal reserve requirements for one type of financial institution and leave the reserve requirements for other financial institutions unchanged.

National institutions have tended to emphasize production loans and investments over trade credits and to be the dominant suppliers of credits to agriculture and, until recent years, the Federal Government. (See Table 16.) Private financial institutions have been the major source of funds for wholesale and retail trade and for mining enterprises. (See Table 17.) In addition, private financial institutions have channeled a substantially larger volume of funds into the industrial sector than the agricultural sector. This is consistent with the growing importance of private *financieras* discussed in Chapter II.

"Interest rates in Mexico seem surprisingly high when one considers the liquidity afforded most securities, the moderateness of inflation in recent years, and the size and diversity of the financial system."[22] Unfortunately, it is not possible to construct a meaningful time series covering interest rates. Rates on government securities have generally been below the prevailing market rate and have been sold to and through the assistance of the Banco de México and other national credit institutions. In the early 1960s, rates of 10 percent to 12 percent on short-term business loans were not uncommon. In 1969, a pamphlet issued by one of the more aggressive and firmly established private *financieras* used the following advertisement to sell securities: "Bonds earn interest at 9.375% ... have always been traded at par in the past and without any deduction for broker's fees or other expenses ... holder receives the principal plus interest earned until the date of sale."[23] This particular *financiera* sold securities in denominations of as little as 1,000 pesos or $80.

Attempts to promote public confidence in private financial institutions has resulted in the extension of many customer services. It is not unheard of for a commercial bank to have a copy of a depositor's signature on file at all of its branches in a particular locality. This and other services necessitate a rather wide spread between the rate that banks pay for money and the rate they charge for it. The extent to which the private financial system has been forced through various monetary controls to

The Financial System

Table 16
Financing Extended by National Credit Institutions, 1942-65[a]
(Millions of pesos)

Year	Total financing	To production Industrial	To production Agricultural	Mining	To trade	To the Federal Government
1942	1,211.4	132.6	318.1	—	13.3	747.4
1943	1,400.3	267.9	375.0	—	23.4	734.0
1944	1,816.0	406.4	518.5	0.1	21.5	869.5
1945	2,226.2	626.8	346.5	0.5	247.8	1,004.6
1946	2,829.0	891.7	421.1	0.8	240.6	1,274.8
1947	3,257.9	1,216.4	542.3	0.9	262.8	1,235.5
1948	4,197.1	1,714.8	535.6	1.0	246.6	1,699.1
1949	5,084.2	2,064.4	631.2	2.6	312.4	2,073.6
1950	5,197.0	2,322.7	723.5	2.7	399.2	1,748.9
1951	6,248.9	3,336.3	732.9	2.8	625.2	1,551.7
1952	6,920.0	3,501.2	985.4	—	668.1	1,765.3
1953	8,289.4	4,274.0	1,392.3	—	572.2	2,050.9
1954	10,524.4	5,717.1	1,418.9	—	751.5	2,654.9
1955	9,872.4	5,025.2	1,799.3	—	533.9	2,514.0
1956	10,352.4	5,061.6	2,132.5	—	1,035.8	2,122.5
1957	11,732.4	5,556.7	2,342.1	—	1,319.7	2,513.9

Table 16 - Continued

Year	Total financing	Industrial	To production Agricultural	Mining	To trade	To the Federal Government
1958	14,759.0	7,266.0	2,708.9	—	1,759.3	3,024.8
1959	16,522.4	8,686.4	3,285.9	—	2,610.3	1,939.8
1960	21,969.4	12,214.6	4,170.8	—	2,878.1	2,705.9
1961	25,897.3	15,541.7	4,828.4	—	3,480.3	2,046.9
1962	29,744.8	20,238.1	5,384.7	—	2,912.2	1,239.8
1963	31,928.9	20,370.7	5,954.0	—	3,059.5	2,544.7
1964	36,123.7	23,504.9	6,476.8	—	3,011.6	3,130.4
1965	42,123.1	23,943.9	7,460.4	—	1,370.7	9,348.1

[a] Adjusted to exclude interbank transactions. Does not include insurance companies.

Source: Data supplied by Gustavo Petricioli, manager of the Banco de México.

Table 17

Financing Extended by Private Credit Institutions, 1942-65[a]

(Millions of pesos)

Year	Total financing	Industrial	To production Agricultural	Mining	To trade	To the Federal Government
1942	812.8	352.0	109.8	6.7	323.3	21.0
1943	1,129.3	452.2	153.5	10.3	478.0	35.3
1944	1,433.9	638.0	207.1	9.2	506.2	73.4
1945	1,849.5	739.1	237.1	8.8	712.0	152.5
1946	2,079.4	910.1	167.3	15.9	848.6	137.5
1947	2,491.0	1,129.5	160.7	14.7	1,022.1	164.0
1948	2,843.7	1,301.8	235.7	14.0	1,137.6	154.6
1949	3,087.8	1,398.1	272.1	14.9	1,234.9	176.8
1950	3,775.7	1,686.9	336.4	23.1	1,411.9	317.4
1951	4,518.4	2,050.6	497.1	23.6	1,682.4	264.7
1952	4,967.5	2,335.1	521.7	20.5	1,878.4	211.8
1953	5,208.4	2,370.4	623.5	21.2	1,865.0	328.2
1954	6,269.0	2,827.7	684.6	44.1	2,400.2	312.4
1955	7,800.3	3,227.3	987.4	57.5	2,856.4	617.7
1956	9,305.2	4,091.3	1,144.8	50.8	3,138.1	880.2

Table 17 - Continued

Year	Total financing	Industrial	To production Agricultural	Mining	To trade	To the Federal Government
1957	10,731.6	4,926.7	1,219.3	60.3	3,414.2	1,111.1
1958	11,824.3	5,343.5	1,289.9	64.4	3,571.5	1,555.0
1959	14,746.6	6,390.3	1,452.6	67.8	4,506.3	2,329.6
1960	17,811.1	7,584.2	1,641.1	62.9	5,585.5	2,937.4
1961	20,158.6	8,882.4	1,754.4	78.5	6,015.0	3,428.3
1962	23,679.6	10,298.1	1,976.0	240.4	6,792.2	4,372.9
1963	29,322.6	12,429.7	2,283.0	213.3	7,983.3	6,413.3
1964	38,311.2	15,195.1	2,841.1	242.7	10,306.6	9,725.7
1965	45,247.4	18,422.8	3,204.3	260.8	12,237.8	11,121.7

[a] Adjusted to exclude interbank transactions. Does not include insurance companies.

Source: Data supplied by Gustavo Petricioli, manager of the Banco de México.

Table 18

Resources of the Private and Public Credit Institutions, 1945-69[a]

(Millions of pesos)

	Private credit institutions	Banco de México	Other national credit institutions
1945	3,765.5	3,416.8	1,003.0
1946	3,939.2	3,240.2	1,331.2
1947	3,164.7	3,285.0	1,640.5
1948	4,681.9	3,826.8	2,182.5
1949	5,134.4	4,414.1	2,850.1
1950	6,796.8	5,620.7	3,242.9
1951	7,661.4	5,934.0	4,267.1
1952	8,460.3	6,320.2	4,826.2
1953	8,885.3	6,688.5	5,952.8
1954	10,554.1	8,693.5	8,841.6
1955	12,947.7	9,009,4	8,208.2
1956	14,817.0	9,935.0	10,521.9
1957	17,236.2	10,428.8	10,983.8
1958	19,583.9	11,328.7	12,634.0
1959	23,186.1	12,332.1	14,647.8
1960	26,716.6	13,204.6	19,544.7
1961	30,335.9	14,587.7	23,052.7
1962	35,254.5	16,074.4	25,844.9
1963	43,183.0	18,373.3	29,697.5
1964	53,895.3	19,928.3	34,425.3
1965	61,598.9	20,723.0	39,205.1
1966	74,420.5	23,329.9	42,904.7
1967	86,206.9	25,707.3	50,463.5
1968	101,276.0	29,844.7	56,896.2
1969	122,824.2	33,501.9	63,797.6

[a]Not adjusted for interbank balances. Does not include insurance companies.
Source: Comisión Nacional de Valores, *Memoria anual, 1964*, pp. 98-99, and Banco de México, *Informe 1965, 1967, 1968, 1969*, pp. 108, 72, 70, and 80, respectively.

finance the public sector at relatively low rates of interest (i.e., holding low-yielding public sector securities as reserves) would limit the supply of funds available to the private sector and generate pressures to regain lost potential returns by charging "higher" rates to private borrowers.

Summary

In terms of resources, Mexico's public and private financial institutions have shown phenomenal growth. (See Table 18.) In 1940, total assets of the private financial institutions amounted to 601 million pesos.[24] By 1969, total assets of the private institutions had expanded over a hundredfold. While the financial system had collapsed following the overthrow of Porfirio Díaz, "by 1960 the Mexican financial system was an efficient, coordinated group of highly diversified institutions which could be mobilized quickly for financing development plans."[25] The private and public systems are integrated in that private institutions have been an important source of funds to the public sector; national institutions, and the Nacional Financiera in particular, have provided financing for private firms; and the Banco de México with support from other national institutions has maintained the liquidity of the financial system. The Nacional Financiera has been instrumental in obtaining large loans from foreign sources to augment the volume of domestic funds. Also, the Nacional Financiera has frequently guaranteed "large sums borrowed from other financial institutions by Mexican firms and agencies, both public and private."[26]

The government has fashioned a number of general and selective monetary controls that enable it to channel funds from private financial institutions to particular sectors of the economy. National credit institutions play a significant role in financing activities that the government considers important for Mexico's development.

While the government has attempted to encourage savings by eliminating the risk of a bank failure and assuring a fixed return on most securities, the highly liquid domestic debt structure imposes a substantial burden on monetary policy to counteract the inflationary potential. Fortunately, the monetary authorities are aware of these problems and are attempting to work out solutions for them.

Notes

1. In the United States, special credit arrangements have been made in regard to agriculture, construction of college or university buildings, and small businesses, among others.

2. See Chapter II, pp. 46-53. Figures published by the Banco de México in its *Informe anual, 1969*, show that *financieras* accounted for 48 percent of the total resources of the private financial institutions, excluding insurance companies. See pp. 82 and 86-87 of the *Informe anual*.

3. See Chapters I and II.

4. El Fondo de Garantía y Fomento a la Industria Mediana y Pequeña would be one example.

5. Hugh T. Patrick, "Financial Development and Economic Growth in Underdeveloped Countries," *Economic Development and Cultural Change* 14 (January, 1966), pp. 175-76.

6. Robert F. Emery, "Mexican Monetary Policy since the 1954 Devaluation," *Inter-American Economic Affairs* 12 (Spring, 1959), p. 73.

7. David H. Shelton, "The Banking System: Money and the Goal of Growth," *Public Policy and Private Enterprise*, edited by Raymond Vernon, p. 115.

8. Frank R. Brandenburg, *The Making of Modern Mexico*, p. 217.

9. The government, through the Nacional Financiera, acquired effective control over the Sociedad Mexicana de Crédito Industrial, a private institution, but has sold it to private interests. This information was obtained in an interview with José Carral, of the Bank of America.

10. Robert L. Bennett, *The Financial Sector and Economic Development*, p. 59.

11. "Mexico Aims to Ensure Bank Independence," *The American Banker*, December 16, 1965, p. 16.

12. *Dilemma of Mexico's Development*, pp. 170-71.

13. Glade and Anderson, p. 156.

14. *Ibid.*, p. 94.

15. Both quotations in this sentence are from Leopoldo Solís M., "Monetary and Financial Policy," *Mexico, a Statist Survey*, January 8, 1965, p. 59.

16. Shelton, p. 122.

17. From a speech by José Hernández Delgado, director general of the Nacional Financiera, entitled "Contribution of Nacional Financiera to the Industrialization of Mexico," delivered to the Mexico City Rotary Club on August 1, 1961, p. 11.

18. "Mexico's Money Men Learn to Lure Capital," *Business Week*, November 26, 1966, p. 117.

19. *Ibid.*

20. Pp. 59-60.

21. Frank M. Tamagna, *Central Banking in Latin America*, p. 169.

22. Shelton, p. 122.

23. Financiera Bancomer, *Investing in Mexico*, p. 7.

24. Shelton, p. 157.

25. Bennett, p. 112.

26. Calvin P. Blair, "Nacional Financiera: Entrepreneurship in a Mixed Economy," *Public Policy and Private Enterprise*, edited by Raymond Vernon, p. 203.

Chapter IV

ECONOMIC GROWTH AND HUMAN WELFARE

Throughout the post-Porfirian period the Mexican Government has struggled to attain some workable balance between promoting rapid economic growth and realizing the social reforms and idealistic humanitarian goals of the Constitution of 1917. While these objectives are interconnected, measures designed to break through one complex of problems restricting the fulfillment of one set of aims have not always advanced the other. The dichotomy has been intensified and complicated because of Mexico's condition—shared by many other states—as an economically less developed nation. Admittedly, some authorities claim that Mexico has already emerged from the less developed category.

"No one any longer doubts that Mexico has the internal human and physical resources, the social organization, and even the level of income which most other countries of the underdeveloped world would be content to achieve thirty or forty years hence."[1] From 1940 to 1968, the compound annual rate of growth in GNP, measured in 1950 pesos, was 6.5 percent. The annual rate of increase in population during this same period was 3.3 percent. (See Table 19.) The rate of expansion in GNP and population from 1958 to 1964, however, was 5.9 percent and 3.5 percent, respectively. On a per capita basis, the gain in GNP during the terms of López Mateos and Díaz Ordaz was at a 2.3 percent and .6 percent rate respectively, compared to a 6.1 percent annual rate during the Ávila Camacho administration. In 1968, the per capita GNP, measured in 1960 pesos, amounted to 5,699 pesos or $456.[2]

The Distribution of Income

The distribution of income has been a subject of great concern to the Mexican Government.[3] President Díaz Ordaz in his first State of the Union message declared:

> No Mexican can enjoy stable prosperity if it is not shared in some measure by all Mexicans. We want to extend and improve the living conditions of our people. We aspire to a little comfort for many Mexicans, reducing the excess of a few. To pledge our greatest efforts

Table 19

GNP, in 1950 Pesos, and Population, 1940-70

	GNP in 1950 prices (Millions of pesos)	Population (Millions of persons)	Per capita GNP (In pesos)
1940	20,721	19.8	1,047
1941	23,289	20.2	1,153
1942	26,373	20.7	1,274
1943	27,358	21.2	1,290
1944	29,690	21.7	1,368
1945	31,959	22.2	1,440
1946	34,084	22.8	1,495
1947	34,517	23.4	1,475
1948	36,080	24.1	1,497
1949	37,627	24.8	1,517
1950	40,577	25.8	1,573
1951	43,621	26.6	1,640
1952	45,366	27.4	1,656
1953	45,618	28.2	1,618
1954	50,391	29.1	1,732
1955	54,767	30.0	1,826
1956	58,214	30.9	1,884
1957	62,708	31.9	1,966
1958	66,177	32.9	2,011
1959	68,119	33.9	2,009
1960	73,482	35.5	2,070
1961	76,038	36.7	2,072
1962	79,691	37.9	2,103
1963	84,700	39.1	2,166
1964	93,200	40.4	2,307
1965	98,200	42.1	2,333
1966	105,600	43.9	2,405
1967	112,400	45.5	2,470
1968	120,400	47.3	2,545
1969*	260,901	47.3	5,516
1970*	279,829	49.1[e]	5,699

Table 19 - Continued

*In 1960 pesos.

^{e}Estimate.

Source: Banco de México, *Informe anual 1961, 1968,* and *1969,* pp. 59, 51, and 53 respectively; Combined Mexican Working Party, *Economic Development of Mexico,* p. 180; Banco Nacional de Comercio Exterior, *Seis años en el comercio exterior de México,* p. 48; Nacional Financiera, *Informe anual 1964 and 1965,* pp. 28 and 31, respectively; and *Business Trends, The Mexican Economy: 1968,* p.33.

Table 20

Distribution of Family Income in Mexico, 1950 and 1957
(Percentages)

Decile	1950 Percent of total income	1950 Cumulative total	1957 Percent of total income	1957 Cumulative total
1[a]	2.7	2.7	1.7	1.7
2	3.4	6.1	2.7	4.4
3	3.8	9.9	3.1	7.5
4	4.4	14.3	3.8	11.3
5	4.8	19.1	4.3	15.6
6	5.5	24.6	5.6	21.2
7	7.0	31.6	7.4	28.6
8	8.6	40.2	10.0	38.6
9	10.8	51.0	14.7	53.3
10	49.0	100.0	46.7	100.0

[a]The 10 percent of the population with the lowest income. Number 10 represents the richest 10 percent of the population.

Source: Ifigenia M. de Navarrete. *La distribución del ingreso y el desarrollo económico de México*, p. 85.

in this direction is to affirm liberty, which ceases to be a privilege and is converted into a genuine right. When men enjoy economic and social security, they can defend it.[4]

A rigorous definitive analysis of changes in income distribution since 1940 would be virtually impossible because of an array of formidable statistical and conceptual problems. These problems include a deficiency in the quantity and quality of necessary data, the difficulties of imputing income for those individuals who are outside the "money" economy, and the vast differences in consumption habits that exist between "low-income" and "high-income" groups and among "low-income" groups living in dramatically different climatic and geographic areas.

In spite of all of these obstacles, several serious efforts have been made to probe the shifts in income distribution over various time periods.[5] While these studies differ somewhat in their approach and methodology, their conclusions generally support the view that the poorest segment of the population may have become relatively poorer.

One study dealing with income, measured in constant 1950 prices, of wage-earning agricultural and nonagricultural workers reported that real wages for both groups declined from 1940 to 1950, but that the decline was noticeably more pronounced among wage-earning agricultural workers.[6] "During 1950 to 1957, the mean family income increased 23 percent in real terms, but is divided in a very unequal form. The lowest 20 percent of the population on the income scale suffered an economic deterioration both relative and absolute..."[7] Table 20 summarizes the shifts in income distribution that are recorded in the study by Ifigenia M. de Navarrete.[8] Table 21 indicates the changes in income distribution that occurred between 1950 and 1964/65.

There is, however, some statistical evidence that labor received a larger share of the national income in 1960 than in 1940.[9] Wages, salaries, and supplements accounted for 29.1 percent of national income in 1940, 23.8 percent in 1950, and 31.4 percent in 1960.[10] Capital, which is defined to include profits, imputed earnings of the self-employed, and rent and interest, claimed 43.9 percent of the national income in 1940, 47.4 percent in 1950, and 42.6 percent in 1960. Mixed incomes, which the Combined Mexican Working Party considered "mostly agricultural earnings but also some profits,"[11] represented 27.0 percent of national income in 1940, 28.0 percent in 1950, and 26.0 percent in 1960.[12]

The available information suggests that those who own and/or manage the largest private enterprises continue to receive the biggest single share of total income but that their share declined several percentage points from 1940 to 1960. The middle and upper-middle classes probably comprised mainly owners and/or managers of medium-sized firms, professionals, higher civil servants, skilled laborers in areas of economic

Table 21

Distribution of Personal Money Income from Wages and Salaries, 1950, 1956, and 1964-65

	Percentage of Income		
Percentage of Persons	*1950*	*1956*	*1964-65*
Lowest 10 percent	3	1	2
Second 10 percent	5	3	2
Third 10 percent	5	4	2
Fourth 10 percent	5	5	7
Fifth 10 percent	7	6	8
Sixth 10 percent	8	7	8
Seventh 10 percent	9	9	8
Eighth 10 percent	11	12	12
Ninth 10 percent	16	16	17
Tenth 10 percent	31	37	36

Source: Jesús Prieto Vázquez, "La distribución del ingreso en México" *Comercio Exterior* 19 (September, 1969), p. 691.

activity that are highly unionized,[13] and owners of large agricultural holdings have increased their share of national income during this period. The unorganized workers, particularly agricultural workers, apparently have suffered a deterioration in their economic position from 1940 to 1960.

Average per capita income varies greatly among states and territories.[14] In general, the standard of living is highest in the Federal District, the two territories of Lower California and the five northern states bordering the United States; it is lowest in Chiapas, Oaxaca, Guerrero, Tlaxcala, Hidalgo, Guanajuato, San Luis Potosí, and Zacatecas. Calculations based on a variety of census data, official statistics published on a yearly basis by various branches of government, and estimates made by the Banco de México indicate that the gap between the richest and the poorest states and territories widened from 1940 to 1960.

The Federal District is, of course, the capital and seat of government. It also is the location of a large part of the nation's industrial complex and receives a heavy yearly inflow of tourist receipts. The seven northern states and territories are also heavily industrialized, at least in comparison with other states. They have a below average percentage of their population in agriculture and have received a greater than average volume of public gross fixed investment expenditures, especially in irrigation projects. In addition, they benefit from their proximity to the United States. The poorer states are characterized by a high proportion of their population working extremely small agricultural plots, unfavorable geographical and/or climatic conditions, and low levels of past public gross fixed investment expenditures.

The Labor Sector of the PRI

The Labor Sector of the PRI has promoted mainly the interests of the industrial workers. The influence of this sector has on a number of occasions been weakened because of strife among various labor leaders for control of the labor movement and the Labor Sector of the PRI. Nevertheless, "labor as opposed to agriculture tends to get a much higher share of political and economic benefits than its numbers warrant."[15]

The membership of labor unions has tended to be concentrated in the larger cities, where labor is far more highly organized than the agricultural population and more accustomed, and willing, to accept internal discipline. During most of the period from 1940 to the present time, the Labor Sector has been dominated by the Confederación de Trabajadores de México (CTM) (Confederation of Mexican Workers). At the present time, the CTM provides leadership and the basic political and economic strength for the Bloque de Unidad Obrera (Labor Unity Bloc), a loose grouping of "moderate" labor unions that constitute approximately 85 percent of the popular membership of the Labor Sector of PRI. The Confederación Revolucionaria de Obreros y Campesinos (Revolutionary Confederation of Workers and Peasants), which was organized in 1952, has tried to provide leadership for the "leftist-oriented" unions within the PRI.

One of the reasons for the success of the organized labor movement is the sweeping, yet specific, guarantees to labor that are incorporated in Article 123 of the 1917 Constitution. The length of the working day, the minimum ratio between rest days and working days, the working conditions for pregnant women, the procedures for establishing legal minimum wages, the rates for the maximum number of hours of overtime, and protection for minors are constitutionally prescribed in a rather detailed manner. The following quotation is an indication of the extent to which the Constitution spells out the rights of labor:

> In every agricultural, industrial, or mining business or any other class of work, the masters *(patrones)* are obliged to provide for their workers comfortable and hygienic habitations, for which they may collect rents which shall not exceed one-half per cent per month of the taxable value *(valor catastral)* of the properties *(fincas)*. Likewise they must establish schools, infirmaries and other services necessary to the community. If the enterprises *(negociaciones)* are situated within towns *(poblaciones)*, and employ a number of workers greater than one hundred, they shall have the first of the obligations mentioned.[16]

Workers are permitted, and in many ways encouraged, to organize. While the Constitution and existing labor laws do not require union membership, they do stipulate employers are to give preference to organized workers. In spite of the incentives to unionize, only a small percentage of the labor force has done so. Of the total labor force, unionized workers constituted 15.0 percent in 1940, 9.9 percent in 1950, and 10.8 percent in 1960.[17] Furthermore, not all unions have been equally successful in winning increased benefits for their members. Thus, the most visible gains that have been achieved by the laboring class have, in fact, been enjoyed by a relatively small number of its members.[18]

Unions must register with the government, and "federal and local authorities, under powers of inspection granted by the Federal Labor Law, have the right to ensure that union funds are administered for the benefit of the members."[19] The close relationship that has developed between the government and union leadership has led one critic to remark: "Labor leaders permitted their unions to become merely one more segment of the Party of the Revolution, that is, of the government party."[20]

The enactment of a compulsory profit-sharing program gives some indication of how the Constitution of 1917 provided a long-range political and economic program that is still in the process of being fulfilled and how the government sought to harmonize diverse viewpoints to establish something approaching a national consensus. While the Constitution laid the groundwork for a compulsory profit-sharing program and there had been some agitation for it—particularly in the early 1950s—legislation implementing this program did not become effective until late 1962.

When President López Mateos first indicated his intention to initiate this program, businessmen, through their various organizations, announced strong disapproval. Labor leaders were enthusiastic. Congress unanimously passed the necessary amendment to the Constitution, which established a commission, whose members were to be appointed by the President, to devise a formula for profit sharing. The states quickly ratified the amendment. The government requested the views of businessmen, educators, and labor representatives concerning this proposal, and the President appointed representatives from management, labor, and finance to the commission. After deliberations, the commission devised a formula which provided:

> for a deduction from net profits after taxes of 30 per cent for dividends and retained earnings, and a variable amount based on the ratio of capital investment to wages and salaries (the higher the ratio, the larger the deduction). From the remainder, 20 per cent must be paid to the workers as their share of profits.[21]

The commission exempted newly organized companies, companies producing new products, firms with net income or net profits below specified levels, and extractive industries during exploratory phases of operations.

While businessmen did not praise the work of the commission, there seemed to be general agreement that its effect would be moderate. Perhaps, a fair summary of the commission's work was provided by one member who stated: "As an average, I would estimate that profit sharing will amount to less than two weeks' pay for employees. Economically it won't break anyone. Psychologically it's important to labor."[22] While the commission stated that profit sharing is to be considered as separate from the concept of wages or other business expenditures, there are no real provisions to prevent businessmen from passing on profit-sharing payments to the consumer in the form of higher prices for goods and services.

Minimum Wage Legislation

From 1933 through 1963, minimum daily wage rates were established biennially by commissions composed of labor, management, and government representatives. In most of the states, minimum wages were set at the *municipio* (similar to county) level, and some *municipios* established different wage levels for various types of work.

The minimum rates for 1964-65 were established by a national commission, also composed of representatives of labor, management, and government. The commission divided the country into 111 zones and was empowered to set minimum rates for various types of work. Studies were conducted in an effort to determine the economic potential of each zone.

Present minimum wage legislation calls for satisfying the minimum social needs, both physical and cultural, of the head of a household. Prior to 1963, minimum wages were theoretically designed to cover minimum essential needs. In response to complaints that the relatively large percentage increases in minimum wages during the last two biennial periods were fostering inflation, the chairman of the Comisión Nacional del Salarios Mínimos offered the following rebuttal:

> The population that benefits [from higher minimum wages] will have greater purchasing power. That population will be able to consume more sugar, bread, and coffee; it will be able to buy a pair of shoes a year, pepper and salt, cloth pants, cotton shirts, and more of other articles. We have surpluses of these articles and export them. As a consequence, there is no inflationary potential. The new minimum wages will indicate the strict application of social justice and never be a cause of inflation.[23]

While the concern for improving the living standard of the masses is understandable, there can be little doubt that increases in minimum wage rates have contributed to inflationary forces. (Table 22 shows average minimum wage rates since 1940.)

The legally established urban and rural minimum wage rates skyrocketed somewhat over tenfold between 1940 and 1965. Inflation, however, advanced at a faster rate than did actual wages between 1940 and 1960. Figures used in a government study of wage rates indicate that real wages dropped from a base of 100.0 in 1940 to 90.8 in 1960.[24]

According to an official of the Secretaría de Industria y Comercio, the average income of all employed persons in 1964 was 15,797 pesos ($1,264).[25] The average for workers who received only the legal minimum was 5,387 pesos ($431), or one-third of the former figure. Furthermore, approximately 40 percent of Mexican workers earned less than the stipulated minimum wage.

The fact that about 40 percent of Mexican workers did not even earn as much as the minimum wage rate reflects the weakness of a limited membership in labor unions. Theoretically, there are no exceptions to minimum wage legislation. Enforcement of minimum wage standards is, however, the responsibility of the state governments, and violations are generally reported by a worker or a union. It is generally assumed that

Table 22

National Average of Minimum Daily Wages in Mexico for Urban and Rural Areas, 1940-65

(Pesos)

Years	Urban	Rural
1940-41	1.52	1.30
1942-43	1.52	1.35
1944-45	1.90	1.65
1946-47	2.48	2.05
1948-49	3.01	2.40
1950-51	3.35	2.66
1952-53	5.32	4.55
1954-55	6.34	5.26
1956-57	7.25	5.99
1958-59	8.13	6.86
1960-61	9.89	8.83
1962-63	12.44	10.92
1964-65	16.95	14.40

Sources: Comisión Nacional de los Salarios Mínimos, *Salarios mínimos: por zonas y municipios, 1964-65*, p. 17; and Nacional Financiera, *50 años de revolución mexicana en cifras*, p. 112.

collective wage agreements are set every two years, after the government establishes new minimum wage rates.[26] This, however, may not be the case in many instances.

Social Security

Mexico's social security program also has its legal base in Article 123 of the 1917 Constitution. While there were a number of studies in regard to establishing a social security program during the presidential terms of Álvaro Obregón, Plutarco Elías Calles, Emilio Portes Gil, and Lázaro Cárdenas, it was in 1942 that President Ávila Camacho sent to Congress the social insurance proposal, which, although amended, is still operative.

The program was started in May 1943 in the Federal District and was slowly extended to other major urban areas. It was not until 1954 that rural workers were brought under the program. Figures published by the Instituto Mexicano del Seguro Social recorded the total number of insured individuals at the end of 1964 at 1,953,300. (See Table 23.) This represented slightly less than 15 percent of the total labor force. The Instituto claims that the total population, including eligible relatives, covered by social security totaled 7,667,704 individuals at the end of 1967.[27]

At first the law provided for:

insurance against 1) accidents on the job and sicknesses resulting from particular types of employment, 2) nonemployment-caused illnesses and pregnancy, 3) disability, old age, and death, and 4) dismissal from employment at advanced age; and in order to organize and cover these branches of insurance, the Instituto Mexicano del Seguro Social was created (by Article 2 [of the Ley de Seguro Social of 1942]). With the reforms promoted by President Adolfo Ruiz Cortines, 1956 marked a new stage by creating the social services which began to fashion, with precision, the Mexican social security system.[28]

The social services that were provided by the reforms of 1956 included medical, educational, and social. In the process of fulfilling these services, hospitals, sanitariums, pharmacies, laboratories, rest homes, family welfare centers, juvenile centers, training centers, and low-cost homes for workers were built by the Instituto. Prior to 1956, the Instituto was able to make payments in services or cash.

In 1959, the social security system was extended to artisans, small businessmen and self-employed professionals, *ejidatarios,* small farmers, and buyers and suppliers for small farmers and *ejidos.* While the number of rural workers insured rose dramatically during the administration of López Mateos, the percentage of insured rural workers to total agricultural

Table 23

Persons Insured by the Instituto Mexicano
del Seguro Social, 1944-67

End of year	Total Persons insured	Urban workers	Rural workers
1944	136,741	136,741	
1945	206,813	206,813	
1946	246,537	246,537	
1947	286,749	286,749	
1948	318,111	318,111	
1949	340,132	340,132	
1950	373,644	373,644	
1951	399,758	399,758	
1952	434,557	434,557	
1953	464,669[a]	464,669	
1954	499,651	497,262	2,389
1955	582,570	571,523	11,047
1956	669,694	650,275	19,419
1957	758,774	734,206	24,568
1958	899,504	871,618	27,886
1959	1,003,779	972,605	31,174
1960	1,180,708	1,153,124	27,584
1961	1,347,129	1,316,362	30,767
1962	1,518,780	1,479,254	39,526
1963	1,767,946	1,627,172	140,774
1964	1,953,300	1,797,622	155,678
1965	2,191,160	1,911,152	280,008
1966	2,315,103	2,028,745	286,358
1967	2,470,425	2,172,668	297,757

[a] On Page 238 of the source this figure, as a result of an obvious typographical error, appears as 466,669. The figure used in this table appears on pages 240 and 241.

Source: Instituto Mexicano del Seguro Social, *La seguridad social en México*, I, pp. 238 and 240-42, and Banco Nacional de Comercio Exterior, *México: 1968*, p. 358.

workers remained quite modest.

The Mexican Government, believing that *ejidatarios* and small private farmers lacked funds to pay the required insurance premiums and that coverage of these groups would tend to raise their living standards, decided to pay a larger portion of their premiums beginning in 1966. Prior to this change, "insurance premiums for maternity, disability, old age, non-job-caused illnesses, dismissal and death have been paid 25 percent by employees, 50 percent by the Government, and 25 percent by employers."[29] As *ejidatarios* and small private farmers have no employer, the government decided to pay 75 percent of their payments. To compensate for these expenditures and to cause a shift of resources to the rural sector, the new regulations require employers to pay 62.5 percent of their workers' premiums and the government to pay 12.5 percent.[30]

As would be expected, the laws have established detailed procedures to calculate the benefits that an insured worker or eligible relative receives under specific circumstances. Periodically upward revisions have been made in the various payment schedules. For example, the minimum monthly old-age pension available to covered workers at age 65 "increased from 30 pesos in 1948 to 50 pesos in 1949, 120 pesos in 1956, and . . . 150 pesos in 1960."[31] For a nonoccupational illness in 1965, cash benefits equal to 60 percent of a qualifying worker's earnings were provided for up to fifty-two weeks.[32] Overall, payment in goods or services rendered have far exceeded payments in money. (See Table 24.) In 1964, almost 88 percent of nonmoney payments which would have included medical, surgical, pharmaceutical, and hospital treatment were registered in the area of non-job-caused illnesses and maternity benefits.[33]

Not all of the social security programs are carried out under the auspices of the Instituto Mexicano del Seguro Social. Civil servants of the Federal Government, the Federal District, Federal Territories, and public agencies incorporated under the Federal Government are covered by the Instituto del Seguro Social al Servicio de los Trabajadores del Estado (ISSSTE). The program of the ISSSTE is similar to that of the Instituto Mexicano del Seguro Social, but it offers additional benefits to government workers. Medical care is provided to government workers, retired employees, and eligible dependents through clinics operated by the ISSSTE. President Díaz Ordaz stated, "Social security benefits were extended to 50 percent more of the population during this administration."[34]

The Government Budget and the Economy

Funds available to the government have always been limited. Until recently, the tax system was cumbersome, highly complex, subject to

Table 24

Total Receipts and Expenditures of the Instituto Mexicano del Seguro Social, 1944-67

(in thousands of pesos)

Year	Total Receipts	Total Expenditures	Nonmoney Payments	Money Payments	Administrative and operational cost
1944	52,923	13,946	8,897	1,844	3,205
1945	60,692	27,641	18,978	3,234	5,429
1946	89,665	46,681	32,978	4,657	9,046
1947	106,466	70,856	49,212	6,127	15,517
1948	142,854	94,518	66,996	7,798	19,724
1949	176,053	126,683	91,150	9,837	25,696
1950	206,268	154,789	109,850	11,637	33,302
1951	253,753	208,510	144,335	15,695	48,480
1952	298,672	260,479	178,269	20,584	61,626
1953	324,477	252,614	173,402	26,320	52,892
1954	384,280	316,892	212,900	33,522	70,470
1955	492,482	375,615	245,471	40,905	89,239
1956	605,948	470,155	299,918	52,212	118,025
1957	855,626	642,289	416,975	84,871	140,443
1958	1,110,677	841,211	524,741	110,010	188,460

Table 24 - Continued

Year	Total Receipts	Total Expenditures	Nonmoney Payments	Money Payments	Administrative and operational cost
1959	1,289,724	1,046,188	676,105	140,893	229,190
1960	1,772,138	1,317,261	829,935	182,981	304,345
1961	2,173,460	1,580,864	987,021	229,711	364,132
1962	2,568,633	1,960,193	1,228,212	284,887	447,094
1963	3,125,749	2,433,821	1,626,692	350,909	456,220
1964	3,715,411	3,020,799	2,077,379	431,930	511,490
1965	4,350,300				
1966	5,122,100				
1967	5,641,300				
1968[a]					

[a]It has not been possible to construct exactly comparable data for more recent years. *México: 1970*, published by Banco Nacional de Comercio Exterior, gives the following breakdown for 1968: income tax, 28.1%; tax on industry, 12.1%; tax on mercantile income, 7.9%; import tax, 10.6%; export tax, 2.9%; other ordinary income, 12.9%; and loans and other finance, 25.5%.

Source: Instituto Mexicano del Seguro Social, *La seguridad social en México*, I, pp. 254-55, and Banco Nacional de Comercio Exterior, *México: 1968*, p. 357.

widespread evasion, and heavily dependent on indirect taxes. Table 25 shows the relative importance of various taxes from 1940 to 1964.

During most of this period, income derived from different sources was subject to varying tax schedules. For example, there were seven separate income tax schedules in 1960. The tax reform of December, 1964, replaced the multiple schedules with "two global categories for personal and corporate income."[35] The main reasons for this major reform were undoubtedly to enhance the government's ability to increase its total revenue, to reduce reliance on indirect taxes, and to strengthen the potential value of the tax system as a tool to redistribute wealth.

The Federal Government's actual budgetary expenditures during the period from 1940 through 1964 averaged 7.9 percent of GNP. (See Tables 26 and 27.) This does not, however, include all of the expenditures of the decentralized government agencies or firms having state participation.[36] In an effort to achieve greater control and coordination of total governmental outlays, it was announced on December 16, 1964, that "more than a dozen semi-autonomous Federal agencies would fall under direct government control in 1965, thus adding their expenditures [which reportedly constituted slightly over 50 percent of the total budget] to the overall budget."[37] It would be extremely difficult, if not impossible, to develop figures showing total expenditures by these agencies from 1940 through 1964 as they had "operated so independently that their books seldom were made public."[38]

If the expenditures of the state, territory, and local governments (adjusted to eliminate double counting resulting from transfers from one level of government to another) are added to the expenditures of the Federal Government, the ratio of government expenditures to GNP would be 2.0 and 2.7 percentage points higher in 1959 and 1964, respectively, than is shown in Table 26.[39] In relative or absolute terms, the outlays of state, territory, and local government units are not unimportant. Mexico's political system, however, is such that these government units are overshadowed and dominated by the Federal Government.

Most local governments do not "have control over their own budgets, which in most states must be approved in the state capital."[40] The state governments in turn are highly dependent on the Federal Government for their revenues[41] and the tenure of their officials. As Frank Tannenbaum has stated: "No governor of a state could be elected against the will of the president or against his known opposition."[42] Furthermore, the President is empowered under Article 76 of the Constitution of 1917 to initiate proceedings to remove state officials.

The omission of the expenditures of the state agencies and firms having state participation would obviously understate the importance of the

Table 25

Receipts of the Federal Government
by Principal Sources, 1940-64

(Percentages)

Tax types	1940	1950	1960	1964
Income	11.4	24.0	33.1	42.0
Import	18.5	12.7	16.0	13.9
Export	9.3	16.3	8.5	5.1
Industrial exercise	16.5	5.0	12.0	12.7
Sales	9.5	14.5	10.0	10.8
Other	34.8	27.5	20.4	15.5

Sources: Combined Mexican Working Party, p. 340, and Banco de México, *Informe anual 1965*, p. 85 and *Informe anual 1961*, p. 53.

Table 26

GNP, Actual Budgetary Expenditures, and Gross Fixed Investment, 1940-69

(Millions of pesos)

Year	GNP	Actual budgetary expenditures of Federal Government	Total gross fixed investment	Gross public fixed investment	Gross private fixed investment
1940	7,000	565	747	290	457
1941	8,800	561	945	337	608
1942	10,700	724	988	464	524
1943	13,700	898	1,227	568	659
1944	17,700	1,117	1,673	657	1,016
1945	20,500	1,354	2,196	848	1,348
1946	26,100	1,415	3,155	999	2,156
1947	29,000	1,767	4,036	1,310	2,726
1948	31,700	2,295	4,456	1,539	2,917
1949	35,200	3,186	5,043	1,956	3,087
1950	40,577	2,850	5,966	2,672	3,294
1951	52,311	4,037	7,513	2,836	4,677
1952	58,643	5,112	8,012	3,280	4,732

Table 26 - Continued

Year	GNP	Actual budgetary expenditures of Federal Government	Total gross fixed investment	Gross public fixed investment	Gross private fixed investment
1953	58,437	4,665	7,676	3,076	4,600
1954	71,540	5,873	9,583	4,183	5,400
1955	87,349	6,575	12,008	4,408	7,600
1956	99,323	7,605	13,631	4,571	9,060
1957	114,225	8,650	15,752	5,628	10,124
1958	127,152	9,677	16,960	6,190	10,770
1959	136,200	10,127	17,476	6,532	10,944
1960	154,137	12,144	20,811	8,376	12,435
1961	163,757	12,929	22,696	10,372	12,324
1962	177,533	14,413	23,528	10,824	12,704
1963	192,200	16,774	27,694	13,821	13,873
1964	224,600	19,888	36,652	17,468	19,184
1965	252,028	n.a.	38,686	16,085	22,601
1966	280,090	n.a.	45,553	21,319	24,234
1967	306,317	n.a.	52,941	24,155	28,786
1968	339,145	n.a.	n.a.	n.a.	n.a.
1969	375,227	n.a.	n.a.	n.a.	n.a.

Table 26 – Continued

Sources: Banco de México, *Informe anual, 1961-69*; Nacional Financiera, *50 años de revolución mexicana en cifras*, p. 136, and *Informe anual, 1961-65*; Ifigenia M. de Navarrete, "El impuesto a las ganancias de capital en la teoría y en la práctica fiscal," *El Trimestre Económico* 30 (April-June, 1963), p. 236; and William E. Cole and Richard D. Sanders, "Income Distribution, Profits and Savings in the Recent Economic Experience of Mexico," *Inter-American Economic Affairs* 24 (Autumn, 1970), p. 61.

Table 27

Ratios of Actual Budgetary Expenditures and Gross
Fixed Investment to the GNP, 1940-67
(Percentages)

Year	Actual budgetary expenditures of Federal Government	Gross public and private investment	Gross fixed public investment	Gross fixed private investment
1940	7.7	10.2	4.0	6.3
1941	6.4	10.7	3.8	6.9
1942	6.8	9.2	4.3	4.9
1943	6.6	9.0	4.1	4.8
1944	6.3	9.5	3.7	5.7
1945	6.6	10.7	4.1	6.6
1946	5.4	12.1	3.8	8.3
1947	6.1	13.9	4.5	9.4
1948	7.2	14.1	4.9	9.2
1949	9.1	14.3	5.6	8.8
1950	7.0	14.7	6.6	8.1
1951	7.7	14.4	5.4	8.9
1952	8.7	13.7	5.6	8.1
1953	8.0	13.1	5.3	7.9
1954	8.2	13.4	5.8	7.5
1955	7.5	13.7	5.0	8.7
1956	7.7	13.7	4.6	9.1
1957	7.6	13.8	4.9	8.9
1958	7.6	13.3	4.9	8.5
1959	7.4	12.8	4.8	8.0
1960	7.9	13.5	5.4	8.1
1961	7.9	13.9	6.3	7.5
1962	8.1	13.3	6.1	7.2
1963	8.7	14.4	7.2	7.2
1964	8.9	15.4	6.9	8.5
1965	—	15.9	6.6	9.3
1966	—	15.0	7.0	8.0
1967	—	15.8	7.2	8.6

Source: Table 26, and especially article by Cole and Sanders for last three years.

Economic Growth and Human Welfare

public sector. The Secretaría del Patrimonio Nacional (Ministry of National Property) reported that the direct contribution of the state agencies and firms having state participation amounted to 6.5 percent of the GNP in 1959, 6.6 percent in 1960, and 7.0 percent in 1961.[43] During these three years, between 74 percent and 78 percent of their contribution represented activity in petroleum, electric power, and transportation and communication.

The direct contribution of the entire public sector to GNP was placed at 9.5 percent in 1959, 11.0 percent in 1960, and 11.5 percent in 1961.[44] The government acquisition in 1960 of most of the remaining private electric industry was responsible for about one-half of the 1.5 percentage point increase in government activity between 1959 and 1960.

An examination of the relationship between public and private gross fixed investment provides a more meaningful insight into the role of the government in the Mexican economy. In this very important area, the government, especially in recent years, has been expanding at a considerably faster rate than has the private sector. During the administrations of Ávila Camacho, Alemán, and Ruiz Cortines, private investment accounted for somewhat over 60 percent of total gross fixed investment. The percentage of private investment fell to 54 percent during the six-year term of López Mateos. While private investment jumped sharply in 1964, it recorded a gain of only 28.8 percent—compared with a spurt of 124.3 percent in public investment—from 1958 through 1963.

As was shown on Table 27, gross public and private fixed investment, except for the last two years of President López Mateos' term, constituted a larger share of GNP during the administration of Miguel Alemán than during any other presidential period. President Díaz Ordaz in his second State of the Union message announced that his program for the remainder of his administration "will require investments of 275 billion pesos; 95 billion from the public sector and 180 billion from the private sector."[45] In his final State of the Union message he announced that total investment authorized for the federal public sector during the 1965-70 period amounted to over 141 billion pesos.

President Díaz Ordaz also stated that increases in internal savings should permit about 90 percent of the projected total gross fixed investment to be financed out of national resources.[46] This has basically been realized. While statistics on domestic savings are quite limited, it has been estimated that from 1950 to 1961 somewhere between 65 percent and 80 percent of private investments were financed by domestic savings.[47]

President López Mateos made a number of statements and pursued certain policies, such as land reform and profit sharing, that created uncertainty as to the extent to which he would have the government intervene in the economy. As a result, businessmen were reluctant to invest at as rapid a rate as they had during the term of Ruiz Cortines. The selection of Gustavo Díaz Ordaz to succeed President López Mateos reputedly was based, at least in part, on his reputation as a moderate and his support within the business community. President Echeverría Álvarez is expected to continue the general policy orientation established by Díaz Ordaz.

Education

The government has given a high priority to education. The Constitution calls for free, compulsory (between the ages of 6 and 14), secular, and socialistic education. The compulsory aspect of the Constitutional mandate has not been achieved. Private educational facilities are permissible, but they must conform to government regulations. The adjective "socialistic" has been dropped.

In 1944, President Ávila Camacho proclaimed an all-out campaign to eliminate illiteracy in Mexico. In 1959, when the program appeared to be faltering, this goal was reaffirmed, and measures were undertaken to attain this educational level by 1970. Since that time, the government has earmarked substantial budgetary resources for education. Commenting on the 1965 budget, one source stated: "As in past years, education received the largest slice of the budget... The education allotment was set at $365,043,600 [U.S. dollars], $40 million more than last year and 23.42 per cent of the total spending."[48] In 1968, the budget of the Public Education Ministry was 59.6 percent higher than its 1964 budget.[49]

Although there was justifiable skepticism that total literacy could have been achieved by 1970, rapid progress has been made in educating the populace, notwithstanding the soaring advances in total and school-age population. The rate of literacy among those six years of age and older rose from 42.0 percent in 1940 to 62.2 percent in 1960.[50] Because of the rapid rise in population, however, the total number of illiterates rose to 10,573,100, or a gain of 1,162,000 persons.

Mexico has a number of public and private universities which permit intensive training in specialized areas. The proximity of the United States affords an opportunity for many students to receive college or graduate school training there. As in many less developed countries, there is some concern that the educational system is producing too many with a broad humanistic or legal background and too few with specialized skills.

The Popular Sector of the PRI

The Popular Sector of the PRI has provided a counterbalance to the interests of the Agrarian Sector and the Labor Sector. When it was first established during the term of President Cárdenas, it afforded a political opportunity for "a considerable number of aggressive individuals outside labor, agriculture, or the government service who were anxious to have a hand in politics and who heretofore had to be blocked from participation by the nature of the party structure."[51] Most of the military heroes are affiliated with the Popular Sector. In addition, it includes teachers, intellectuals, women's groups, youth groups, a variety of civic or betterment groups, small farm proprietors, and all but the highest echelon of state employees. These disparate groups are organized into one of ten branches of the Confederación Nacional de Organizaciones Populares, which attempts to coordinate the activities of the Sector.

To a large extent, the Popular Sector represents the desires and aspirations of the middle and upper-middle income groups. It has benefited from the political astuteness and relatively high educational level of its individual members. Since the Administration of President Ávila Camacho, the Popular Sector has probably been the most dominant sector.[52]

There have been complaints that the sector is dominated by the Federación de Sindicatos de Trabajadores al Servicio del Estado, which by law includes all government workers except the high administration officials appointed by the President and workers in the areas of electric power, petroleum, railroads, and social security. The federation, however, has argued that it should be a sector by itself.

Summary and Conclusions

The Mexican Government has played a major role in the country's developmental process. While there has never been an official national economic plan such as the various five-year plans of the U.S.S.R., the government has been moving toward the fulfillment of the economic and social program expounded in the 1917 Constitution. In some areas, the government has expanded its influence beyond that envisioned by the original document. In other areas, objectives outlined in the Constitution are far from realization.

While the government has had a substantial impact on the economic process and has far-reaching importance within the economic system, Mexico's economy cannot accurately be termed socialistic. The major theoretical expositions on socialism called for its development from a full-fledged capitalistic state.[53] The concept that a country could reasonably pursue a socialistic course without first achieving the necessary economic base presupposed by capitalism emanated largely from the fertile, pragmatic, and, in some ways, flexible mind of Lenin. It was not until the Twenty-second Party Congress that a Soviet leader maintained that the U.S.S.R. had succeeded in building a socialistic economy.

Mexico in its present stage of development does not meet many of the underlying assumptions of the capitalistic model. Because of the limitations of its domestic market, one or a very few suppliers of various commodities could regulate the price of a given product. The institution of private property exists but is subject to whatever regulations the government may impose in the name of the public interest. In many cases, individuals and firms are willing to restrict the horizons of income or profit maximizations for nationalistic objectives such as Mexicanization of industry.

While Mexico's economy does not duplicate the capitalistic model, it must be stated that no economy ever has. The capitalistic model is an extremely useful intellectual abstraction that has functioned perfectly only in the minds of men. Mexico, however, deviates substantially further from the basic assumptions of this model than did the economies of the United States, Great Britain, and the states of Western Europe at the turn of the century. The categorization of Mexico as a less developed country obviously indicates that in theory and practice Mexico has not yet attained the economic foundation presupposed by the capitalistic model.

The trends from 1940 to the present indicate that Mexico has been developing toward a mixed economy which relies heavily upon the government to assure "social justice" and to promote economic growth. Profit sharing, social security, land reform, and minimum wage legislation have been clearly designed to further humanitarian aims. Nationalization, heavy outlays for fixed investment, the creation of specialized national credit institutions, and tariff protection were undertaken primarily in hopes of promoting economic growth.

Some measures such as price controls have been pictured as attempts to create, by government intervention, the results that would have occurred in a competitive market. Certainly, the keen interest to form some workable Latin American Common Market indicates the government's awareness of the importance of expanding Mexico's market. Balance-of-payment pressures have recently brought about a re-evaluation of the extent to which self-sufficiency should be a national goal and the margin of protection that can be justified for existing industries. Apprehension over sustaining a rapid rate of economic growth has resulted in a lively debate on the wisdom of forcing the Mexicanization of industry. Thus, the competitive model has served as a guide in policy making.

Mexico appears to be reaching a particularly important stage in the development of its economic system. Land for redistribution is virtually exhausted, but the rural population continues to expand. Government officials speak of closing the income gap between the rich and the poor, but there has been no program to curtail the growth in population. Promotion of import substitution programs have led to substantial increases in industrial production; but further stimulus from this area may be quite limited unless Mexico can enlarge its markets. Furthermore, there is considerable question in regard to the benefits that could be expected from a Latin American Common Market.

The major problems confronting Mexico are not new. In 1950, Sanford A. Mosk stated:

> the size of the internal market, the supply of capital and credit, the training of labor, technicians, and management, the tendency toward inflation, and the balance of payments. These are the major problems, and they suggest the bottlenecks that are likely to be prominent in Mexico as the industrialization process goes forward.[54]

Of course, Mexico's population explosion was another factor that should have been listed.

While these bottlenecks have been quite troublesome in the past and will continue to be so in the future, Mexico has been wrestling with all of these issues, except the growth in population. If there is a change in the official position of the Roman Catholic Church in regard to birth control, the government would be more likely to undertake some program to limit future population growth. Government officials and most economists, however, have been silent on the issue of population control.

In his inaugural address on December 1, 1970, President Luis Echeverría Álvarez went so far as to rule out birth control openly.

At the present time, Mexico has a national economy that has achieved a degree of self-sustaining growth. It has a vigorous private sector that owns the lion's share of the means of production, and the government by reducing protection against imports is subjecting the private sector to increasing foreign competition. The country has a relatively sophisticated financial community, a good international credit rating, and a program of extensive and intensive education.

While the President of Mexico has almost dictatorial power during his six-year term, he has a definite responsibility as leader of the PRI to maintain the support of all segments of the population. It is not an easy matter politically to change policies that have shielded Mexican businessmen and laborers from the effects of foreign competition or that have gained acceptance as genuine national goals. The strength of Mexican nationalism,[55] coupled with the understandable unwillingness of certain businessmen and laborers to meet foreign competition, is a definite restraint against the rapid removal of protective devices. Dramatic shifts in agricultural policy are unlikely because of the possibility of alienating a large and important segment of the population.

The balance between public and private efforts that will be utilized to solve Mexico's problems is uncertain and relies on many "ifs." Past experience would suggest that Mexico will follow a rather pragmatic approach, with the government concentrating its resources in developing the country's infrastructure. Private industry will continue to own most of the country's means of production, but the government will undoubtedly continue to influence the actions of the private sector. Overall, government policy will probably continue to stress increasing production rather than attempt to force a major redistribution of income of wealth.

Notes

1. Raymond Vernon, *The Dilemma of Mexico's Development*, pp. 5-6.

2. In current prices, per capita GNP amounted to 7,642 pesos, or $611, in 1968.

3. In discussions with private citizens in a variety of occupations and with government officials, some who requested that they not be named or directly quoted, expressed to me their concern with the potential difficulties and instability that they considered to be inherent in any system where marked disparity exists between "the rich" and "the poor." Following is a summarization of their point of view:

> Mexico must be seen in its historical context. Many people think of Mexico as a "showcase" for economic development. We have made progress, but we are aware of many problems. There is a wide disparity between the rich and the poor, and this gap has been widening. If the people lost faith that we were working to better their position, all of us who are washed and well groomed could be killed tomorrow. You need only ride through the poorer sections of the cities or through the countryside to realize that we are sitting on a powder keg. We must do many things that are not "economic" to keep people satisfied. We overstaff to make jobs and force investments into certain areas when market pressures would direct funds in other ways. For example, some people have pointed out that certain areas of Mexico are ideally suited for cattle raising. They are right, and we know it. We don't invest much in cattle raising because it does not create as many jobs as other, less productive, uses of the land.

> Please do not misunderstand us. We do not
> expect a revolution, but you must realize that
> many of our economic policies are designed to
> assure continued economic stability and not to
> maximize productivity. (The United States is
> undertaking such measures in regard to its black
> population.)
>
> For years officials have kept one eye closed to
> our Constitution, a great social document, but
> slowly we are achieving the goals it espoused.
> Right now we are working toward goals that will
> not be accomplished for about fifty years. For-
> tunately, even the poorest Mexicans have faith
> that their children will have greater opportuni-
> ties and a better life than they have had. Those
> of us in positions of responsibility must keep
> that faith alive.

I must also point out that every younger Mexican — roughly all those under 40 — that I spoke with expressed shock and disbelief that anyone could conceive of the possibility of a violent revolution in Mexico.

    4. *Comercio Exterior* 15 (September, 1965), p. 632.

    5. Some writers have sidestepped the basic question of income distribution and have discussed statistical data or observations which indicated that the living conditions of the poorer groups have improved but have omitted trends and developments relating to the income or wealth of the well-to-do. See Vernon, pp. 93-94.

    6. Miguel Flores Márquez, *La distribución del ingreso en México*, p. 7, as cited in Raymond G. Conatser, "Land Reform and Economic Development: Mexico 1930-1960," pp. 99-100.

    7. Ifigenia de Navarrete, *La distribución del ingreso y el desarrollo económico de México*, p. 95.

    8. After appraising the various major studies on in-come distribution in several Latin American countries, a 1964 United Nations study entitled *The Economic Development of Latin America in the Post-War Period*, p. 64, states

that the Navarrete book is "the most systematic and consistent investigation."

9. The information in this paragraph is taken from "Los salarios y el desarrollo económico," *Revista de Economía* 26 (December, 1963), pp. 343-50.

10. The return to labor mentioned here refers to a much broader universe than the lowest 20 percent of the population on the income scale mentioned in the preceding paragraph.

11. *Economic Development of Mexico*, p. 7.

12. Many economists seriously doubt that the statistics on income distribution accurately reflect the full amount of income received by labor. William E. Cole and Richard D. Sanders, however, state, "The relatively small share of Mexican national income 26.3 percent in 1966 going to wages and salaries is not atypical of Latin American countries." See "Income Distribution, Profits and Savings in the Recent Economic Experience of Mexico," *Inter-American Economic Affairs* 24 (Autumn, 1970), p. 50.

13. The following section discusses the status of unions and unionized workers in the Mexican economic system.

14. The following two paragraphs are based on material from Paul Lamartine Yates, *El desarrollo regional de México*.

15. Robert E. Scott, *Mexican Government in Transition*, p. 74.

16. Joseph Wheless, *Compendium of the Laws of Mexico*, p. 67. The Price Waterhouse booklet *Information Guide for Doing Business in Mexico* also discusses worker benefits.

17. "Los salarios y el desarrollo económico," *Revista de Economía* 26 (December, 1963), p. 349.

18. See following section.

19. Arthur Neef, *Labor Law and Practice in Mexico*, p. 32.

20. Octavio Paz, *The Labyrinth of Solitude: Life and Thought in Mexico*, p. 180.

21. Board of Governors of the Federal Reserve System, "A Bit-O-Honey for Labor," *Latin American Economic Developments*, February 28, 1964, p. 2. The report of the commission was reprinted in *Comercio Exterior* 13 (December, 1963), pp. 882-87.

22. James C. Tanner, "Mexico Plans Yule Gift for Workers: Bonuses Companies Must Pay," *Wall Street Journal*, December 5, 1963, p. 1.

23. "Fijación de salarios mínimos," *Comercio Exterior* 13 (December, 1963), p. 898.

24. "Los salarios y el desarrollo económico," *Revista de Economía* 26 (December, 1963), p. 349.

25. The data in this paragraph are taken from Sergio Luis Cano, "Política de salarios y distribución del ingreso," *Comercio Exterior* 15 (September, 1965), p. 634.

26. Adolf Strumthal, "Economic Development, Income Distribution, and Capital Formation in Mexico," *Journal of Political Economy* 63 (June, 1955), p. 193.

27. Banco Nacional de Comercio Exterior, *México: 1968*, p. 358.

28. Benito Coquet, *La seguridad social en México*, I, p. 21.

29. "Higher Social Security Tax in Mexico," *Financial Times*, December 29, 1965, p. 14.

30. *Ibid.*

31. Neef, pp. 60-61.

32. *Ibid.*, p. 59.

33. Calculated from Table 6 and data provided in *La seguridad social en México*, I, p. 261.

34. State of the Union address (September, 1970), p. 12b.

35. David F. V. Ashby, "Mexico -- Model for Latin America?" *The Banker* 115 (August, 1965), p. 538.

36. It does include transfer from the federal government to these agencies.

37. "New Administration in Mexico Creates Record 1965 Budget," *New York Times,* December 17, 1964, p. 17.

38. *Ibid.*

39. Nonfederal government expenditures were computed from Banco de México, *Informe 1961*, pp. 120-21, and *Informe 1965*, pp. 150-51. Ifigenia M. de Navarrete, using the same concept of government expenditures but apparently working with certain figures which have since been revised and not adjusting for intergovernmental transfers, indicates that the ratio of federal, state, and local governmental expenditure to GNP was 11.3 in 1940 and 11.8 in 1960. She also included net expenditures for some decentralized agencies and firms having state participation. See "Hacia una política impositiva para el desarrollo," *Política fiscal de México*, p. 177. Data provided for the 1939-51 period in the report of the Combined Mexican Working Party, *Economic Development of Mexico*, p. 338, show the same general picture but with still another set of ratios.

40. Scott, *Mexican Government in Transition*, p. 46.

41. Industrias e Inversiones Alba, *Mexican Tax Digest: A Supplement to 'Investor's Mexican Letter'* (1958), p. 4, states: "A high proportion of state and municipal expenses is in fact met from participation in federal tax revenues and federal grants-in-aid."

42. Frank Tannenbaum, *Ten Keys to Latin America,* p. 167.

43. Secretaría del Patrimonio Nacional, *1962 Report on Decentralized Agencies and State Participation Enterprises* p. 62f.

44. *Ibid.*, p. 44.

45. *Comercio Exterior* 16 (September, 1966), p. 649.

46. *Ibid.*

47. Dwight S. Brothers, "El financiamento de la formación de capital en México," *Comercio Exterior* 13 (December, 1963), p. 907.

48. "New Administration in Mexico Creates Record 1965 Budget," *New York Times*, December 17, 1964, p. 17.

49. Banco Nacional de Comercio Exterior, *México: 1968*, p. 375.

50. Computed from *Revista de Estadística* 28 (July, 1965), p. 766.

51. Vernon, *Dilemma of Mexico's Development*, p. 129.

52. Frank R. Brandenburg, "Mexico: An Experiment in One-Party Democracy," pp. 234-87.

53. Karl Marx, of course, was the first theoretician to develop fully the concept that a socialistic state would emerge from a capitalistic state, but he had predecessors, such as Sismondi, Saint-Simon, Richard Jones and others, who helped evolve this idea. See Henryk Grossman, "The Evolutionist Revolt against Classical Economics," *Essays in Economic Thought: Aristotle to Marshall*, edited by Joseph J. Spengler and William R. Allen (Chicago: Rand McNally, 1960), pp. 500-24. Joseph A. Schumpeter in his *History of Economic Analysis* (New York: Oxford University Press, 1954), p. 763, wrote that "one need not be a Marxist in order to realize that the private enterprise system tends to develop toward a socialistic form of organization."

54. *Industrial Revolution in Mexico*, p. 304.

55. Manning Nash in his perceptive article "Economic Nationalism in Mexico," in *Economic Nationalism in Old and New States*, states on p. 83: "It [nationalism] energized and gave purpose to the strivings of large numbers of Mexicans, and at the same time allowed them to forego immediate returns in favor of the larger end of Mexicanidad."

BIBLIOGRAPHY

Adie, Robert F. "Cooperation, Cooptation, and Conflict in Mexican Peasant Organizations." *Inter-American Economic Affairs* 24 (Winter, 1970): 3-25.

American Banker (New York), 1963-69.

Andic, Fuat M. "El desarrollo económico y la desigualdad en el ingreso: El caso de México." *El Trimestre Económico* 30 (July-September, 1963): 375-81.

Ashby, David F. V. "Mexico — Model for Latin America?" *The Banker* (London) 115 (August, 1965): 532-38.

Asociación de Banqueros de México. *Anuario financiero de México*. Mexico City: 1962-69.

Aubey, Robert T. *Nacional Financiera and Mexican Industry*. Los Angeles: Latin American Center, University of California, 1966.

Baerresen, Donald W.; Carnoy, Martin; and Grunwald, Joseph. *Latin American Trade Patterns*. Washington, D.C.: Brookings Institution, 1965.

Banco de México. *Informe*. Mexico City: 1962-69.

Banco Nacional de Comercio Exterior. *Informe*. Mexico City: 1960-69.

──────. *México: 1960, México: 1963, México: 1966, México: 1968, and México: 1970.*

──────. *Seis años en el comercio exterior de México*. Mexico City: 1964.

Barlow, Edward R. *Management of Foreign Manufacturing Subsidiaries*. Boston: School of Business Administration, Harvard University, 1953.

Beltrán, Enrique et al. *México: Cincuenta años de revolución*. 4 vols. Mexico City: Fondo de Cultura Económica, 1960-62.

Bennett, Robert L. *The Financial Sector and Economic Development: The Mexican Case*. Baltimore: Johns Hopkins Press, 1965.

Beteta, Ramón. *Tres aspectos del desarrollo económico de México*. Mexico City: Publicaciones Especializadas, Sección de Economía, 1963.

Betts, Virgil. *Central Banking in Mexico*. Ann Arbor: University of Michigan Press, 1957.

Blanksten, George I. "The Politics of Latin America." In *The Politics of the Developing Areas*, edited by Gabriel A. Almond and James S. Coleman. Princeton: Princeton University Press, 1960.

Braithwaite, Stanley N. "Real Income Levels in Latin America." *Review of Income and Wealth*, series 14 (June, 1968): 113-82.

Brandenburg, Frank R. "A Contribution to the Theory of Entrepreneurship and Economic Development: The Case of Mexico." *Inter-American Economic Affairs* 16 (Winter, 1962): 3-23.

———. *The Development of Latin American Private Enterprise*. Washington, D.C.: National Planning Association Pamphlet no. 121, 1964.

———. *The Making of Modern Mexico*. Englewood Cliffs, N. J.: Prentice-Hall, 1964.

———. "Mexico: An Experiment in One-Party Democracy." Ph.D. dissertation, University of Pennsylvania, 1955.

Business Week, 1965-70.

Bibliography

Carrillo Flores, Antonio. *El desarrollo económico de México.* Mexico City: Banco de México, 1950.

Carroll, Thomas F. "The Land Reform Issue in Latin America." In *Latin American Issues: Essays and Comments,* edited by Albert O. Hirschman. New York: Twentieth Century Fund, 1961.

Centro de Estudios Monetarios Latinoamericanos. *Los mercados de capital en América Latina.* Mexico City: 1966.

"Changing Wage Structure: An International Review." *International Labor Review* 73 (March, 1956): 273-83.

Christian Science Monitor, 1964-70.

Civil Code for the Federal District and Territories of Mexico, and the Mexican Laws on Alien Landownership. Translated by Otto Schoenrich. New York: Baker, Voorhis, 1950.

Cole, William E., and Sanders, Richard D. "Income Distribution, Profits and Savings in the Recent Economic Experience of Mexico." *Inter-American Economic Affairs* 24 (Autumn, 1970): 49-63.

Comisión Nacional Bancaria. *Memoria estadística.* Mexico City: 1952-61.

Comisión Nacional de Valores. *Memoria anual.* Mexico City: 1961-69.

Conatser, Raymond G. "Land Reform and Economic Development: Mexico 1930-1960." Ph.D. dissertation, Southern Methodist University, 1965.

Coquet, Benito et al. *La seguridad social en México.* 5 vols. Mexico City: Instituto Mexicano del Seguro Social, 1964.

Correo Económico (Mexico City), 1966-70.

Departamento de Asuntos Agrarios y Colonizaciones. *Seis años de política agraria del Presidente Adolfo López Mateos: 1958-1964.* Mexico City: 1964.

Eckstein, Salomón. *El marco macroeconómico del problema agrario mexicano.* Mexico City: Centro de Investigaciones Agrarias, 1968.

Economist (London), 1963-70.

Eder, George Jackson. "Urban Concentration, Agriculture, and Agrarian Reform." *Annals of the American Academy of Political and Social Sciences* 360 (July, 1965): 68-77.

Emery, Robert F. "Mexican Monetary Policy since the 1954 Devaluation." *Inter-American Economic Affairs* 12 (Spring, 1959): 72-85.

Faltermayer, Edmund K. "We're Bullish on Mexico." *Fortune* 72 (September, 1965): 149-264.

Fernández y Fernández, Ramón. "El seguro agrícola." *Estudios Agrarios* 1 (January April, 1961): 53-78.

———. *Economía agrícola y reforma agraria.* Mexico City: Centro de Estudios Monetarios Latinoamericanos, 1962.

——— and Acosta, Ricardo. *Política agrícola.* Mexico City: Fondo de Cultura Económica, 1961.

Financial Times (London), 1965-70.

Flores, Edmundo. *Tratado de economía agrícola.* Mexico City: Fondo de Cultura Económica, 1961.

Flores Márquez, Miguel. *La distribución del ingreso en México.* Mexico City: 1958.

García Duarte, Alberto. *Problemas económicos de México.* Mexico City: 1966.

Glade, William P., and Anderson, Charles W. *The Political Economy of Mexico.* Madison: University of Wisconsin Press, 1963.

González Navarro, Moisés. "Mexico: The Lop-sided Revolution." In *Obstacles to Change in Latin America,* edited by Claudio Veliz. London: Oxford University Press, 1965.

Bibliography

González Santos, Armando. *La agricultura: Estructura y utilización de los recursos.* Mexico City: Fondo de Cultura Económica, 1957.

Goodspeed, Stephen. "The Role of the Chief Executive in Mexico: Politics, Powers and Administration." Ph.D. dissertation, University of California at Berkeley, 1947.

Gordon, Wendell. *The Political Economy of Latin America.* New York: Columbia University Press, 1965.

Harrar, Jacob G. *The Agricultural Program of the Rockefeller Foundation.* New York: Rockefeller Foundation, 1956.

―――. *Mexican Agricultural Program.* New York: Rockefeller Foundation, 1950.

Hernández Delgado, José. *The Contribution of Nacional Financiera to the Industrialization of Mexico.* Mexico City: Nacional Financiera, 1961.

Himes, James R. "La formación de capital en México." *El Trimestre Económico* 32 (January-March, 1965): 153-79.

Hoover, Calvin B., ed. *Economic Systems of the Commonwealth.* Durham: Duke University Press, 1962.

―――. "The Relevance of the Competitive, Laissez-faire Economic Model to Modern Capitalistic National Economies." *Kyklos,* fasc. 1 (1955): 40-58.

International Bank for Reconstruction and Development, Combined Mexican Working Party. *The Economic Development of Mexico.* Baltimore: Johns Hopkins Press, 1953.

Kling, Merle. *A Mexican Interest Group in Action.* Englewood Cliffs, N. J.: Prentice-Hall, 1961.

Kuznets, Simon et al. *El ingreso y la riqueza.* Mexico City: Fondo de Cultura Económica, 1963.

La Cascia, Joseph. *Formación de capital y desarrollo económico en México*. New York: Praeger Special Studies, 1969.

Lees, Norman E. *Localización de industrias en México*. Mexico City: 1965.

López Romero, Adolfo, and Colín Trejo, Eduardo. "Modelo macroeconómico simple para la economía mexicana." *El Trimestre Económico* 32 (October-December, 1965): 725-47.

Manero, Antonio. *La revolución bancaria en México*. Mexico City: Talleres Gráficos de la Nación, 1957.

Manne, Alan S. "Key Sectors of the Mexican Economy, 1960-70." In *Studies in Process Analysis*, edited by Alan S. Manne and Harry M. Markowitz. New York: Wiley, 1963.

Martínez de Escobar, Rafael. *How to Do Business in Mexico*. New York: Exposition Press, 1961.

McClelland, David C. "Does Education Accelerate Economic Growth?" *Economic Development and Cultural Change* 14 (April, 1966): 257-78.

Mendieta y Núñez, Lucio. *El problema agrario de México*. 7th ed., rev. Mexico City: Porrúa, 1959.

Mexican Business Council. *Mexico: 1970-1976*.

Molina, Julian B. *A Statement of the Laws of Mexico: In Matters Affecting Business*. 2d ed. Washington, D.C.: Pan American Union, 1955.

Moore, Ernest. *Evolución de las instituciones financieras en México*. Mexico City: Centro de Estudios Monetarios Latinoamericanos, 1963.

Moreno Sánchez, Manuel et al. *Política ejidal*. Mexico City: Universidad Nacional Autónoma de México, 1960.

Mosk, Sanford A. *Industrial Revolution in Mexico*. Berkeley: University of California Press, 1950.

Nacional Financiera. *Informe*. Mexico City: 1960-68.

———. *El mercado de valores*. Mexico City: 1960-71.

———. *Nacional Financiera en el desarrollo económico de México, 1934-1964*. Mexico City: 1964.

Nash, Manning. "Economic Nationalism in Mexico." In *Economic Nationalism in Old and New States*, edited by Harry G. Johnson. Chicago: University of Chicago Press, 1967.

Navarrete, Alfredo. *Instrumentos de política financiera*. Mexico City: Publicaciones Especializadas, 1964.

Navarrete, Ifigenia de. *La distribución del ingreso y el desarrollo económico de México*. Mexico City: Universidad Nacional Autónoma de México, 1960.

———. *Política fiscal de México*. Mexico City: Universidad Nacional Autónoma de México, 1964.

Neef, Arthur. *Labor Law and Practice in Mexico*. Washington, D. C.: U. S. Department of Labor, Bureau of Labor Statistics Report no. 240, 1963.

New York Times, 1962-70.

Noticias (New York), 1965-70.

Orive Alba, Adolfo. *La política de irrigación en México*. Mexico City: Fondo de Cultura Económica, 1960.

Ortega Mata, Rolfo. "Metas de la seguridad social en la aceleración del desarrollo." *Revista Mexicana de Sociología* 26 (September-December, 1964): 715-48.

Ortiz Mena, Raúl et. al. *El desarrollo económico de México y su capacidad para absorber capital del exterior*. Mexico City: Nacional Financiera, 1953.

Owen, Wyn F. "The Double Development Squeeze on Agriculture." *American Economic Review* 56 (March, 1966): 43-70.

Parks, Richard W. "The Role of Agriculture in Mexican Economic Development." *Inter-American Economic Affairs* 18 (Summer, 1964): 3-27.

Patrick, Hugh T. "Financial Development and Economic Growth in Underdeveloped Countries." *Economic Development and Cultural Change* 14 (January, 1966): 174-89.

Paz, Octavio. *The Labyrinth of Solitude: Life and Thought in Mexico.* Translated by Lysander Kemp. 2d ed., rev. New York: Grove Press, 1961.

Presidencia de la República, Secretaría Privada, and Nacional Financiera. *50 años de revolución mexicana en cifras.* Mexico City: 1963.

Prieto Vázquez, Jesús. "La distribución del ingreso en México." *Comercio Exterior* 19 (September, 1969): 686-96.

Price Waterhouse. *Information Guide for Doing Business in Mexico.* June, 1968.

Rice, Katherine E. *Basic Data on the Economy of Mexico.* Washington, D. C.: U. S. Department of Commerce, World Trade Information, pt. 1, no. 59-5, Economic Reports, January, 1959.

Rockefeller Foundation, Director's Annual Report. *Mexican Agricultural Program.* New York: 1954-55, 1958-59.

Rodríguez Adame, Julián. *Reforma agraria y progreso agrícola.* Mexico City: 1959.

Rodríguez Mannch, Juan. "Los ejidatarios, los comisariados ejidales y el crédito." *Estudios Agrarios* 2 (January-April, 1962): 27-37.

Rosas Figueroa, Aniceto, and Santillán López, Roberto. *Teoría general de las finanzas públicas y el caso de México.* Mexico City: Universidad Nacional Autónoma de México, 1962.

Rottenberg, Simon. "México: Trabajo y desarrollo económico." *Foro Internacional* 2 (July-September, 1961): 85-112.

"Los salarios y el desarrollo económico." *Revista de Economía* 26 (December, 1963): 343-50.

Schultz, Theodore W. "Latin-American Policy Lessons." *American Economic Review* 46 (May, 1956): 425-32.

Scott, Robert E. *Mexican Government in Transition.* 2d ed., rev. Urbana: University of Illinois Press, 1964.

Secretaría de Agricultura y Ganadería et al. *Projections of Supply of and Demand for Agricultural Products in Mexico to 1965, 1970, and 1975.* Translated by the Israel Program for Scientific Translations. Jerusalem: 1966.

Secretaría de Economía. *Memoria.* Mexico City: 1950-51 and 1958.

Secretaría de Gobernación. *Seis anos de actividad nacional.* Mexico City: 1946.

Secretaría de Industria y Comercio. *Comercio Exterior.* Mexico City: 1963-69.

―――. *Memoria de labores.* Mexico City: 1960, 1961, and 1959-69.

―――, Departamento de los Censos. *Censos agropecuarios* (1930, 1940, and 1950). Mexico City: 1959.

―――, Dirección General de Estadística. *IV censos agrícola-ganadero y ejidal, 1960.* Mexico City: 1965.

―――. *VII censo industrial: 1960, resumen general.* Mexico City: 1965.

―――. *Revista de Estadística.* Mexico City: 1964-66.

Secretaría del Patrimonio Nacional. *1962 Report on Decentralized Agencies and State Participation Enterprises.* Mexico City: 1962.

Secretaría de la Presidencia, Dirección de Inversiones Públicas. *México: Inversión pública federal, 1925-63.* Mexico City: 1964.

Seligman, Daniel. "The Maddening, Promising Mexican Market." *Fortune* 53 (January, 1956): 103-76.

Senior, Clarence O. *Land Reform and Democracy*. Gainesville: University of Florida Press, 1958.

Siegel, Barry N. *Inflación y desarrollo: Las experiencias de México*. Mexico City: Centro de Estudios Monetarios Latinoamericanos, 1960.

Silva Herzog, Jesús. *El agrarismo mexicano y la reforma agraria*. 2d ed. Mexico City: Fondo de Cultura Económica, 1964.

Solís M., Leopoldo. "Cambios recientes en la estructura y comportamiento de la economía mexicana." *Investigación Económica* 30 (January-March, 1970): 23-70.

Statist (London), 1963-67.

Strumthal, Adolf. "Economic Development, Income Distribution, and Capital Formation in Mexico." *Journal of Political Economy* 63 (June, 1955): 183-201.

Tamagna, Frank M. *Central Banking in Latin America*. Mexico City: Centro de Estudios Monetarios Latinoamericanos, 1965.

Tannenbaum, Frank. *Mexico: The Struggle for Peace and Bread*. New York: Knopf, 1950.

———. *Ten Keys to Latin America*. New York: Knopf, 1962.

Tucker, William P. *The Mexican Government Today*. Minneapolis: University of Minnesota Press, 1957.

United Nations. *Statistical Yearbook*.

———, Economic Commission for Latin America. *The Economic Development of Latin America in the Post-War Period*. E/CN.12/659/Rev.1. New York: 1964.

United States, Department of Agriculture, Foreign Agricultural Service. *Land Distribution in Mexico*. FAS-N112. Washington, D.C.: 1961.

Bibliography

———, Department of Commerce. *International Commerce.* Washington, D. C.: 1963-70.

———, Department of Commerce. *Investment in Mexico.* Washington, D. C.: 1955.

——— Social Security Administration, Division of Program Research. *Social Security Programs throughout the World, 1958.*

Universidad Nacional Autónoma de México, Escuela Nacional de Economía. *Nuevos aspectos de la política económica y de la administración pública en México.* Mexico City: 1960.

Vernon, Raymond. *The Dilemma of Mexico's Development.* Cambridge: Harvard University Press, 1963.

———, ed. *Public Policy and Private Enterprise in Mexico.* Cambridge: Harvard University Press, 1964.

Walter Thompson de México. *The Mexican Market.* 2d ed. Mexico City: 1963.

Waterston, Albert. *Development Planning: Lessons of Experience.* Baltimore: Johns Hopkins Press, 1965.

Wheless, Joseph. *Compendium of the Laws of Mexico.* 2d ed., rev. St. Louis: Thomas Law Book Co., 1938.

Yates, Paul Lamartine. *El desarrollo regional de México.* 2d ed. Mexico City: Banco de México, 1962.

INDEX

Acosta, Ricardo, 22, 33n
Agrarian Reform Act, 27
Agrarian Sector of the PRI, 6-7, 26, 105
Agricultural credit banks, 16, 17, 18
Aguilar, Luis, 58
Alemán, Miguel, 3, 16, 18, 22, 32n, 68, 103
Almacenes Nacionales de Depósito, 25
Anderson, Charles W., 32n, 60n, 62n, 63n, 80n
Anderson-Clayton Company, 71
Article 27 (of Constitution), 1
Article 28 (of Constitution), 21
Article 76 (of Constitution), 97
Article 123 (of Constitution), 88, 92
Ashby, David F. V., 63n, 113n
Asociación de Banqueros de México, 21, 34n, 68
Asociación Nacional de Cosecheros, 7
<u>Atribuciones</u> del <u>Ejecutivo en Materia Económica</u>, 25, 40
Avila Camacho, Manuel, 3, 18, 22, 68, 92, 103, 104, 105
Azcárraga, Emilio, 58

Bailleres, Raúl, 58
Ballentine, Douglas K., 61n
Banco Hipotecario Urbano y de Obras Públicas, 63n

Banco de México, 10n, 20n, 21, 23n, 45n, 50, 52n, 53, 65, 66, 67, 68, 70n, 71, 72, 77n, 78, 79n, 83n, 87, 98n, 101n, 113n
Banco Nacional Agropecuario, 18, 21
Banco Nacional de Comercio Exterior, 10n, 17, 23n, 31n, 32n, 63n, 83n, 93n, 96n, 112n
Banco Nacional de Crédito Agrícola, 17, 21, 65
Banco Nacional de Crédito Ejidal, 17, 21
Banco Nacional de Fomento Cooperativo, 63n
Banco Nacional de Transportes, 63n
Barlow, Edward R., 62n
Barovick, Richard L., 62n
Beans, 22, 24
Bennett, Robert L., 71, 79n, 80n
Blair, Calvin P., 63n, 64n, 80n
Blanksten, George I., 30n
Bloque de Unidad Obrera, 87-88
Brandenburg, Frank R., 30n, 31n, 32n, 33n, 58, 63n, 64n, 79n, 114n
Brothers, Dwight S., 114n

Calles, Plutarco Elías, 3, 65, 92

Cámara Nacional de la Industria de Transformación, 37
Campos Salas, Octaviano, 34n
Cannon Mills, 71
Cano, Sergio Luis, 112n
Cárdenas, Lázaro, xii, 2, 3, 4, 11, 36, 43, 92, 105
Carral, José, 3n, 79n
Carranza, Venustiano, 3
Cement, 35, 46
Central American Common Market, 39
Chiapas, 87
Cole, William E., 101n, 102n, 111n
Comisión Nacional Bancaria, 66, 67, 68
Comisión Nacional de los Salarios Mínimos, 29n, 90, 91n
Comisión Nacional de Valores, 66, 68, 70n, 77n
Comité de Aforos, 21
Comité Regulador del Mercado de las Subsistencias, 21
Comité Regulador del Mercado del Trigo, 21
Compañía Distribuidora de Subsistencias Populares, 22
Compañía Exportadora e Importadora (CEIMSA), 17-18, 21, 22, 37
Compañía Maíz Industrializado, 22, 25
Compañía Nacional de Subsistencias Populares (CONASUPO), 21-22
Compañía Rehidratadora de Leche, 22
Conatser, Raymond G., 28n, 29n, 110n
Confederación de Cámaras Industriales (CONCAMIN), 36, 37
Confederación de Cámaras Nacionales de Comercio (CONCANACO), 36, 37
Confederación Nacional Campesina, 6, 30n
Confederación Nacional de Organizaciones Populares, 105
Confederación Nacional de la Pequeña Propiedad Agrícola, 7
Confederación Patronal de la República Mexicana 37
Confederación Revolucionaria de Obreros y Campesinos, 88
Confederación de Trabajadores de México (CTM), 87
Constitution of 1917, 1, 28n, 81, 88, 89, 92, 97, 104, 105
Construction, 10, 35, 44-45
Coquet, Benito, 112n
Cotton, 4, 17

Diario Oficial, 2
Díaz, Porfirio, 41, 65, 78
Díaz Ordaz, Gustavo, 1, 2, 3, 4, 6, 18, 25, 27, 30n, 34n, 39, 42, 46, 61n, 68, 81, 94, 103, 104
Dirección General de Precios, 25, 26
Durán, Marco Antonio, 33n

Echeverría Alvarez, Luis, 27, 61n, 104, 107
Education, 4, 104
Ejidatarios, xiii, 2, 4, 11, 17, 21, 22, 29n, 30n, 92, 94
Ejidos, 2-6, 11, 26, 27, 28n, 92
Electric power, 10, 35, 43, 44-45, 46, 47-49, 53, 55, 58, 103, 105
Emery, Robert F., 79n
Espinosa Yglesias, Manuel, 42
Exports, 22, 25, 39
Expropriation, 2, 4

Index

Faltermayer, Edmund K., 29n, 62n
Federación de Sindicatos de Trabajadores al Servicio del Estado, 105
Federal District, 40, 87, 92, 94
Fernández y Fernández, Ramón, 22, 29n, 33n
Financieras, 50, 65, 72, 79n
Flores, Edmundo, 3n, 29n
Flores Márquez, Miguel, 110n
Fondo de Garantía y Fomento para la Agricultura, Ganadería y Avicultura, 21
Fondo de Garantía y Fomento a la Industria Mediana y Pequeña, 53, 57, 79n
Forestry, 5, 9, 10, 12-13

García family, 58
Garza Sada family, 58
Giniger, Henry, 30n, 62n
Glade, William P., 32n, 60n, 62n, 63n, 80n
GNP, 7, 10, 35, 81, 82-83, 97, 99-100, 102, 103, 113n
Goethals, Henry W., 61n
Gómez, Rodrigo, 21, 33n
González Navarro, Moisés, 29n
González Santos, Armando, 16, 29n, 32n
Guajardo, G. Xavier, 29n
Guanajuato, 87
Guerrero, 87

Harrar, Jacob G., 31n
Henequen, 4, 28n
Hernández Delgado, José, 80n
Hidalgo, 87
Hoover, Calvin B., xi, xiii, xv
Huerta, Adolfo de la, 3

Imports, 22, 37, 38, 40, 41, 58, 107

Instituto Mexicano del Seguro Social, 92, 93, 94, 95-96
Instituto del Seguro Social al Servicio de los Trabajadores del Estado, 94
International Bank for Reconstruction and Development, Combined Mexican Working Party, 31n, 32n, 35, 60n, 83n, 85, 98n, 113n
Investments, 7, 11, 12-14, 16, 18, 27, 35, 42, 46, 53, 71, 99-100, 102, 103, 104
Iron, 35, 46, 47-49, 56
Irrigation, 2, 11, 12-13, 15, 16, 27, 28n, 31n, 46, 87
Izquierdo, Rafael, 62n

Kennedy, Paul P., 30n

Labor, 7, 8, 35, 36, 85, 87, 88, 89, 90, 91, 92, 93, 94, 105, 107
Labor Sector of the PRI, 6, 7, 87-89, 105
Latin American Common Market, 39, 106, 107
Latin American Free Trade Area, 39
Ley de Fomento de Industrias de Transformación, 37-38
Ley de Industrias de Transformación, 37
Livestock, 12-13, 18, 20n
López Mateos, Adolfo, 2, 3, 4, 18, 22, 43, 68, 81, 89, 92, 103, 104

Maize (Corn), 16, 17, 22, 24, 25
Manufacturing, 10, 44-45
Martínez de Escobar, Rafael, 61n
Marx, Karl, 114n

Mendieta y Núñez, Lucio, 29n
Mexicanization, 41-43, 71, 106
Michoacán, 4
Milk, 22, 25
Mining, 10, 35, 42, 43, 44-45, 47-48
Monterrey, 58
Moore, Ernest, 32n, 34n
Moreno Sánchez, Manuel, 29n
Mosk, Sanford A., 53, 107

Nacional Distribuidora y Reguladora, 18, 21
Nacional Financiera, xvn, 9n, 15n, 24n, 30n, 50, 53, 54-56, 64n, 66, 70n, 78, 79n, 80n, 83n, 91n, 101n
Nash, Manning, 114n
Nationalization, 42, 43-46, 106
Navarrete, Ifigenia M. de, 84n, 85, 101n, 110n, 111n, 113n
Neef, Arthur, 60n, 111n

Oaxaca, 87
Obregón, Alvaro, 3, 65, 92
Ollervides, Paul A., 62n
Orive Alba, Adolfo, 31n
Ortiz Rubio, Pascual, 3
Owen, Wyn F., 33n

Pagliai, Bruno, 58
Pan American Union, 34n
Parks, Richard W., 30n
Partido Revolucionario Institucional (PRI), 6, 7, 36, 87, 88, 104, 107
Patrick, Hugh T., 79n
Paz, Octavio, 112n
Petricioli, Gustavo, 74n, 76n
Petroleum, 10, 35, 43, 44-45, 46, 47-49, 103
Popular Sector of the PRI, 6, 7, 104-105
Population, 4, 42, 46, 59, 92, 107

Portes Gil, Emilio, 3, 92
Price Waterhouse, 111n
Prices, 21, 22, 25, 26, 27, 39, 41, 106
Prieto Vázquez, Jesús, 86n

Rice, 4, 17, 22
Rice, Katherine E., 31n, 62n
Rocha, Joel, 58
Rockefeller Foundation, 16
Rodríguez, Abelardo, 3
Rodríguez Mannch, Juan, 29n
Ruiz Cortines, Adolfo, 3, 18, 22, 68, 92, 103, 104
Ruiz Galindo, Antonio, 58

Sanders, Richard D., 101n, 102n, 111n
Scott, Robert E., 30n, 60n, 111n, 113n
Secretaría de Economía, 25, 26, 34n, 38
Secretaría de Hacienda y Crédito Público, 41, 53, 66
Secretaría de Industria y Comercio, 5n, 9n, 25-26, 29n, 39, 40, 41, 53, 60n, 62n, 63n, 90
Secretaría del Patrimonio Nacional, 53, 103, 113n, 114n
Secretaría de la Presidencia, 14n, 31n, 49n, 60n
Secretaría de Recursos Hidráulicos, 11
Seligman, Daniel, 62n
Shelton, David H., 63n, 79n, 80n
Sociedad Agronómica Mexicana, 6
Sociedad Mexicana de Crédito Industrial, 79n
Solís M., Leopoldo, 80n
Steel, 35, 43, 46, 47-49, 53
Strumthal, Adolf, 112n

Tamagna, Frank M., 80n
Tannenbaum, Frank, 97, 113n
Tanner, James C., 62n, 112n
Taxes, 37, 38, 42, 94, 97, 98
Textiles, 35, 53
Tlaxcala, 87
Transportation and communication, 10, 35, 43, 46, 47-49, 103
Trouyet, Carlos, 58
Tucker, William P., 30n, 31n

United States Department of Agriculture, 29n, 31n, 34n
U.S.S.R., 105, 106

Vernon, Raymond, xvn, 26, 33n, 34n, 60n, 62n, 63n, 68, 109n, 114n

Waterston, Albert, 63n
Wheat, 4, 16, 17, 21, 22, 24
Wheless, Joseph, 28n, 33n, 111n
Wionczek, Miguel S., 62n
World War II, xii, 18, 35, 37, 41, 65

Yates, Paul Lamartine, 30n, 111n
Yucatan peninsula, 4

Zacatecas, 87

SOC
HC
135
R58